Pet Tales

Pet Tales

Extraordinary Pets From Ordinary Homes

The Telegraph

with a foreword by
Ben Fogle

CONSTABLE · LONDON

CONSTABLE

First published in Great Britain in 2013 as *Charmers and Rogues*
by Constable, an imprint of Constable & Robinson Ltd.
This paperback edition published in 2015 by Constable

A CIP catalogue record for this book
is available from the British Library.

ISBN 978-1-47212-268-1 (paperback)

1 3 5 7 9 8 6 4 2

Typeset in Great Britain by SX Composing DTP, Rayleigh, Essex
Printed and bound in Great Britain by CPI Group (UK) Ltd, Croydon CR0 4YY

Papers used by Constable are from well-managed
forests and other responsible sources

MIX
Paper from
responsible sources
FSC® C104740

Constable
is an imprint of
Little, Brown Book Group
Carmelite House
50 Victoria Embankment
London EC4Y 0DZ

An Hachette UK Company
www.hachette.co.uk

www.littlebrown.co.uk

Your Receipt

REGINA
PUBLIC
LIBRARY

Customer ID: ************0280

Items that you checked out

Title: Pet tales : extraordinary pet tales from
  ordinary homes
ID: 39085901839635
Due: December-11-21

Total items: 1
Nov-13-2021 14:24
Overdue: 0

Enjoy your materials! Late fines will not be
charged, but consider donating any fines you
may have paid to the library. Explore digital
services, live online programs, and branch
hours at www.reginalibrary.ca

REGINA PUBLIC LIBRARY

Support your library.
Reginalibrary.ca/donate

REGINA PUBLIC LIBRARY

Support your library.
Reginalibrary.ca/donate

CONTENTS

INTRODUCTION

'Real-life Lassie saves elderly woman from
freezing ditch'.

'Kitten eats TV aerial'.

'Cat who travelled 1,700 miles trapped in the
undercarriage of a train has lost a leg and at
least one life but will soon be home' . . .

THERE HAS NEVER been a shortage of pets making the headlines
for acts of heroism or extreme misfortune. Yet stories of
everyday domestic animals were never deemed important
enough to be told in print. The only chance a lovable moggy,
devoted dog or mildly eccentric chicken had of making it into
the papers would be if their owner was a talk-show host or a hat
designer to royalty.

It was decided there was to be a 'pets' corner' in the Life
section of the Sunday Telegraph. We had toyed with a pet health
column, but fleas, overeating and furballs were already covered
by the excellent Pete Wedderburn in Weekend. We tried a pet
behaviour Q&A for dogs who chewed up the house and cats
who refused to eat unless they were hand-fed fresh prawns.
But it lacked a certain something. We were looking for a light,
endearing column which revealed the foibles, funny turns and,
above all, unbridled joy pets gave their owners.

Who better to write this column than the Telegraph readers
themselves? We had to get the ball rolling, and so we tracked

down staff members known to have pets. No one was safe. I accosted a page designer and owner of a cat, Lupin ('Call me Lupin . . . Reader, I carried him' remains one of my favourites). Our deputy editor volunteered his West Highland White terrier, Pixie, and in doing so revealed what an utter pushover he was. A reluctant dog owner, he was quickly floored by Pixie's charms and his 'downfall' recorded with glee by his young daughters. There was even a snake who belonged to the young son of Telegraph cartoonist Matt Pritchett, kindly submitted by his wife Pascale. Charlie the corn snake would rear up like a 'very angry pencil', and appears in the 'Escape Artists' chapter with good reason. To this day Charlie may still reside under the floorboards of the family's former house. Indeed, Matt contemplated whether to mention Charlie in the fixtures and fittings inventory.

With a couple of tales in print and an invitation to readers to submit their own entries, the first few began to arrive in early 2010. A rescue greyhound was, appropriately, first out of the traps. A substantial number of tales come from owners who adopt a rescue animal. Some have experienced brutal homes: Benjy the Yorkie/Jack Russell cross was found cowering under a table; Poppy, Georgie and Tally the Patterdale terrier and her two puppies were discovered running along the dual carriageway, and were easily parted from their cruel owner for hard cash. Some came from abroad: Bonzo, the skeletal pointer puppy found in Northern Cyprus; Aslan, the deaf cat, in Greece; and Henri the duck in a French market, who was surely facing l'Orange.

There are tales of dramatic survival against the odds. Jackson the dachshund was attacked in Richmond Park by a deer with no sense of fair play. Parsley the cat was caught in an illegal gin trap, had his right front leg amputated but lived to twenty-one years old. And Flint, the mighty Great Dane, had a heart condition which weakened his back legs, but he battled on with the aid of a chariot, running over the foot of anyone who got in the way.

Lovable Rogues, of whom there are many, evoke the greatest loyalty and admiration in their owners. A Labrador called the Honourable Hannah gatecrashed a photo opportunity with the Queen Mother and broke royal protocol with an overt display of affection. Then there is the irrepressible Billy Bob the spaniel, who failed his obedience class in spectacular fashion. Pets can be abominably behaved and we will adore them all the more. Mussolini the duck returned from an emergency trip to the vet and was soon 'back to his repulsive self', explained his owner, adding: 'I wouldn't have it any other way.'

The chapters are a mix of species and breeds because I don't believe only a 'cat person' would enjoy a tale about cats. Admittedly, and unsurprisingly, there is a preponderance of cats in the 'Pampered Charmers' chapter – the owner of Tamby, former BBC newsreader Jan Leeming, explains it well when she says: 'You own a dog, but a cat owns you.' The 'Joy Givers', however, are mostly dogs, but every pet in this book arguably belongs in this category (with the exception, perhaps, of Charlie the corn snake).

Do I have a favourite? For me it has to be Tina the bear, who belonged to Sir Peter Whiteley. Sir Peter served in the military and was based in Singapore in the sixties, where exotic pets seemed to be quite the thing. When he was eventually posted to another country, Tina had to go to a zoo. 'I have had many wonderful dogs as pets,' said Sir Peter, 'but Tina the bear was quite exceptional.'

It has been a pleasure to make this selection. The editing of Pet Tales has always been kept to a minimum because these are stories from the heart, and beautifully written. You would have to be made of stone not to be moved by the tale of Dexter the spaniel, Rosie the Labrador or Barclay the golden retriever. The 'Dearly Departed' chapter is one of poignant eulogies to fallen friends, some long gone but never to be forgotten.

What is evident from this little book of stories is that pets give us back so much more than we ever hoped for. They are the face that is always pleased to see us, the individual who never judges, the reason to get out of the house and the reason to come home again. They are a soothing presence, a sympathetic companion, the best friend. They have helped owners cope with divorce, illness, grief, even death.

The dictionary definition of a pet is 'a tame animal kept for companionship and amusement'.

I don't think that quite covers it.

Anne Cuthbertson

FOREWORD

by Ben Fogle

Inca, black Labrador

INCA WAS MY shadow: loyal, funny, naughty and loving. She brought light and laughter to my life. As every owner will say, she was so much more than just a dog; she was my best friend. She brought me more joy, happiness and laughter in her twelve years than anyone else I know. Stealing cakes, chewing the post and raiding the bin, I loved her for her foibles. Her absolute love of food, her unstoppable dribbling and her snoring were all part of what made me love her. And she loved me. Despite my long absences over the years, she was always there. Tail wagging, happy to see me. Never upset, annoyed or angry with me. She was a constant in a chaotic and varied life.

We spent the first year of her life together marooned on a deserted island in the Outer Hebrides. For the social experiment that was the BBC's Castaway, each of us was allowed one luxury item and I chose a puppy. Ever since, she became a sort of guardian angel, unknowingly helping shift and shape my life. It was Inca who helped me get my first presenting job in wildlife, and she went on to be my silent co-host on dozens of shows from Crufts to Countryfile.

Perhaps her biggest coup, though, was helping find me a wife. Marina and I met while we were walking our dogs in the park. Inca and Maggi, Marina's Labrador/collie cross became best friends, and we became husband and wife. Iced marzipan figures of Inca and Maggi adorned the top of our wedding cake, and our honeymoon involved a pilgrimage with the new Mrs Fogle and dogs to the Outer Hebrides, where it all began.

When Inca's tired body finally failed, I lay on the floor and wept uncontrollably into her thick fur. My father, a vet, injected her and as I felt her heart stop beating, I let out a guttural sob.

Inca, Inca Pinka, the Stink, Stinky . . . we had so many names for her. When I think of her I smile. It's been quite a trip, me and Inca, the best friend I ever had.

I am thrilled that Inca's story joins the many enchanting, moving and funny tales in this book.

Ben Fogle, London 2013

PART ONE

LOVABLE ROGUES

Billy Bob, puppy-preschool failure

Having been a stoutly cats-only household for some time, the hurricane-like arrival of Billy Bob, the golden cocker spaniel, came as a collective shock.

As the biggest puppy of his litter, with an aptitude for sitting on his brethren like an irate sumo wrestler, the writing was on the wall. As were two of our three cats, within seconds of his arrival. The third fled up the chimney, and was coaxed down only through a mix of tense negotiations, darkness and copious amounts of salmon.

A measure of calm was achieved, but only after Billy Bob was allowed to colonize and terrorize the back of the house, hijacking the washing from the line and chomping his way through it like a demented moth.

Our cats repaired indignantly to the front, and plotted the downfall of the big-eared monster. It had all the territorial hallmarks of Woody Allen and Mia Farrow's living 'apart together' arrangement.

Evidence of Billy Bob's capacity to deploy 'shock and awe' tactics without warning came on his first day at 'puppy preschool'. A dozen pups of varying shapes and sizes fidgeted as owners sat in a semicircle trying in vain to exert a modicum of control.

Billy Bob appeared to be above it all and adopted a strangely passive, seated Buddha pose. He then ruined it by rugby-tackling the paddling pool in the centre, noisily depositing the contents of his bladder into it. He failed preschool but did receive a certificate, albeit without a schedule of training events.

He is now nearly ten, but while his power naps are longer, his energy and capacity to create mayhem are largely undiminished. Our remaining cat, Ben, is nineteen; he has tamed the beast by becoming just as mad. They are the classic odd couple.

LIKES squirrels, baguettes, not owning a built-in satnav
DISLIKES commands, his bed, the elevated location of cat food
FINEST HOUR dressing up as a soft ice cream by eating the duvet

Gordon McDowall, London

Chubbs, magnificently malevolent tabby

CHUBBS IS a tabby with attitude. His real name is Admiral Lord Seymour of the Bridge, and we often wonder if our alternative title for him has contributed to the roll call of bleeding limbs, torn slippers and empty wallets that have haunted us for the past seven and a half years, or if he was just born a wicked, furry bag of razors.

He is about nine years old and has mellowed. We can roll over in bed without being mauled, and you can walk past him without risk of a lightning paw strike.

Of course, you say, they've spoilt him! And you would be right. You see, he is disabled – with only three legs. How this happened neither we, nor the cat home where we got him, will ever know.

Not a weekend goes by without a tasty treat or a new collar or a fluffy companion making an appearance – all to no avail. Chubbs is determined to hate the world. He refuses to be groomed and can't be bothered to do it himself, so he is sedated by the vet every May and combed out.

Our food budget is skewed – a fortune on prime cuts for him and scrag-end for us. Christmas is a nightmare: he refuses to be enticed with Father Christmas suits or rhinestone collars. He will partake of some turkey, but only skinless breast.

Cats congregate in neighbouring gardens to yowl and gossip about him. He is so furious that we have squatted in his home that the only way to stop his anger is to force upon himself a sleep pattern that would put a corpse to shame – all night on the bed and all day on a (red velvet) cushion.

In our dreams he is loving and dependent; we spend a lot of time dreaming. Chubbs is invincible. He is magnificent. He is our lad.

LIKES kipping
DISLIKES everything else
FINEST HOUR executing a martial-arts manoeuvre on our neighbours' Siamese cat, which threw her into the garden pond

Karen Morgan, Surrey

The Honourable Hannah

WE CALLED her The Honourable in the hope that it might make her better behaved than her fellow Labradors, Jemima and Rebecca. All in vain, as it proved.

As a puppy she was seen chasing a large rabbit around the rose bed. But as Hannah got farther and farther away from the rabbit, and the rabbit closer and closer to Hannah's tail, we realized that the roles were reversed: Hannah fled in through the French windows and, trembling, sought refuge in her bed.

On another occasion, a friend, a distinguished French scholar, lent me a series of books on the history of France in beautifully leather-bound and gilded covers. Hannah had evidently become bored with mere chair and table legs to chew, and decided that one of these volumes had possibilities.

Fortunately I arrived before there was too much damage,

but we had to find a good bookbinder, who took his time over a long and expensive repair. Sadly, during this time, my friend died. I approached his widow with profuse apologies. 'It can't be helped,' she replied, 'and what excellent taste in literature your puppy has.'

For six months we had been used to Hannah's arrival home covered in mud. We assumed she had been taking revenge on the rabbits by digging up their warren. How wrong we were.

I walked up to the church one morning, where the rector was gossiping with the sexton by the lychgate. As I reached them, out from the churchyard ran a very muddy Hannah bearing what was unmistakably a human thigh bone in her mouth. 'My goodness,' exclaimed the rector, 'not another Resurrection.'

We searched and searched, but never found where the reinterment had taken place.

Many years ago on the occasion of her visit to Jersey, the late Queen Elizabeth the Queen Mother had lunch with us and afterwards consented to a photograph in the garden. Jemima, now mature, was allowed in the photo, while the two young ones were shut in the house. Or so we thought.

As we stood ready in front of the camera, out from the house rushed Hannah, who seated herself adoringly at the Queen Mother's feet. Then, at the very moment the shutter clicked, Hannah landed a very wet and loving kiss on the Queen Mother's right hand.

Before I could do anything to repair the damage, the Queen Mother bent over and wiped her hand on Hannah's head. 'Thank you, dear,' she said, 'but do you mind having it back?'

Sir Peter Whiteley, Devon

Mussolini, conniving duck

I AGREED to Mussolini and his two sisters coming to us in a moment of weakness. I felt sorry for him, and although we had chickens, we did have room. We bought him a plastic sandpit for a mini-pond, and some additional companions (he is pictured here with Daffy, his main consort).

But his unpleasant nature manifested itself swiftly. He positively enjoyed mistreating the additions to his harem. Captain Mainwaring, our other Muscovy pure-bred male, is pompous but charming. Mussolini is sly.

A short time ago, I returned from work at lunchtime to find Mussolini badly entangled in the netting around my one remaining respectable flower bed. His efforts to free himself had made matters worse and he was thrashing around. I immediately cut him free, but his chest was badly lacerated so I stuck him into the cat carrier while he tried to peck my fingers, and rushed him to the vet. The wonderful Grant from Lady Dane Vetinary Centre sucked in his breath as Mussolini looked balefully at us both, all the time dripping blood, and said he needed stitches and antibiotics as well as Metacam. I opened my mouth to say 'duck à l'orange, then', and caught Mussolini's eye. Reader, I could not do it to him.

Several days of nursing in a rabbit cage followed, with my lugubrious husband squirting antibiotic while I tilted the duck's head to get the medicine down. We took down the netting and replaced it with a duck-proof fence. For a while I thought he might not make it, as he refused all efforts to get him to eat – even the worms I dug were spurned.

The course of antibiotics finished and he limped out to sun himself. I hovered in case the rest of the birds attacked him, but they did not dare. We had turned the corner. He is back to his repulsive self. I wouldn't have it any other way.

LIKES duckweed and dominating females
DISLIKES being handled and shows of affection
FINEST HOUR seeing off Schnapps the cat

Stephanie Wolfe, Faversham

Flossie, danger to postmen

FLOSSIE CAME to live with us when she was five years old. Her owners had sold her because she was too energetic, excitable and noisy, and they had a Weimaraner to look after as well; apparently, together they were causing havoc.

They warned us that Flossie was so anarchic that she needed to be an only dog. But we had kept pairs of Jack Russells before, and were confident that we could manage her, even though we also had another old fellow called Scrumpy. The vendors looked doubtful.

As soon as we got her home, she proceeded to demolish Scrumpy's favourite toy, a string of squeaky sausages, and to bully him. She was extremely territorial, not letting people in the gate and barking furiously at anyone who dared walk past our house. We were forced to fit a new six-foot gate and an outside mailbox to satisfy the postman. We also put up a large 'enter at own risk' sign.

One day, her previous owners rang to ask how she was. We

had to be honest: terrible! However, she had already wormed her evil way into our hearts.

Although she loathed everyone else, she adored us, and our two sons. When they came in, she would throw herself into paroxysms of hysterical affection, even if they had only been out for ten minutes!

Now that dear old Scrumpy is deceased, Flossie is finally an only dog, and is happily ruling the roost. Despite her shortcomings, we are devoted to her and she to us.

LIKES chocolate drops and tombstoning
DISLIKES postmen, passers-by, other dogs
FINEST HOUR finally ruling the roost

Alice Selley, Exeter

Pixi, feline terrorist

THE VET was surprised that Pixi willingly wolfed down the activated charcoal that she was about to be force-fed. We weren't.

At five months old, it was already hard to imagine the tranquil life we had enjoyed PP (Pre-Pixi). A life where lie-ins at the weekend were uninterrupted, and things were generally where you left them and not inside her stomach.

Potential cat owners beware. The sleepy ball of black fluff at the shelter enchanted us: we had to have her. But cats are clever. Once home, she was transformed into a feline terrorist, destroying all around her.

The curtains were first to be targeted, and suffered irreparable damage. Newspapers, books and letters were shredded, chewed and digested, and television cables severed. The jar of cotton buds (used to a quiet life on the bathroom shelf) came under constant attack, and buds disappeared at an alarming rate.

Various techniques were employed to ensure we did not sleep too long. Most effective was the 'water-flick' – a paw dipped into a carelessly placed glass of water by the bed and flicked on to our weary faces.

The first bunch of flowers I received from my boyfriend in two years sparked the charcoal incident (a costly error, not since repeated). Terrorist feline bided her time. Once alone, she knocked over the vase and ate the flowers. Lilies, as it turns out, can be lethal if eaten by cats.

We rushed her to the vet's, where she remained for three days as we worried whether she would live to wreak havoc again – £500 later we brought Pixi home.

The house had been horribly quiet and empty without her.

LIKES eating (anything), cotton buds, climbing and cables
DISLIKES the wind
FINEST HOUR surviving the dreaded lilies

Jenni Williams, St Albans

Samson, destroyer of expensive clothing

WE ALMOST came home with a different dog: my husband preferred the puppy that was nibbling his shoes to the one that crept on to my lap and promptly fell asleep. However, Samson, as we later named him because of his long hair and dissident ways, was determined we didn't leave without him.

The first night he arrived, we put him to bed in the utility room and he whined. We tried to ignore it. The second night the whining got louder. The third, we tucked a hot-water bottle in beside him and the whining stopped. He had obviously been missing the comfort of his mother.

Samson is often asked to do party tricks when we have visitors. He will bark on command, find lost toys and offer his paw when you say, 'Gimme five'. His latest skill is to play dead, but it doesn't last for long when he spots a treat as a reward. Perhaps he's not ready for *Britain's Got Talent* quite yet.

We wondered how Samson would react when he was taken

to the vet for the first time. We thought he might be timid, scared even. However, he must be the only dog who positively shakes with excitement upon reaching the vet's door. He bounds over to the desk, puts his paws up on the counter and begs to be spoilt by the receptionist.

On one occasion, we took him to stay at a relative's house. Thinking that he would be fine in the kitchen with the other two dogs, a few minutes later we heard a crash and rushed through to find one of the kitchen chairs on the floor. Lying next to it was a very expensive goose-down jacket with the pockets ripped out. All three dogs were innocently sitting on their rugs. We looked over at Samson, who, despite seeming as though butter wouldn't melt in his mouth, had a feather sticking out of the side of his muzzle.

We often say that Samson came to us at exactly the right time. He has been a comforting companion in the midst of loss and grief. We were a bit hesitant about getting a dog at first, but now we wouldn't have it any other way. Samson is one of a kind.

LIKES going to the vet, staying at the boarding kennels, hugs
DISLIKES the garden hose, the hoover
FINEST HOUR lying very still while our two-year-old niece pulled his ears, tickled his nose and snuggled in beside him

Valerie MacInnes, Ross-shire, Scotland

✳ ✳ ✳

PART TWO

TIMID SOULS

Digger, nervous Airedale

'WELL, YOU did name him Digger,' said the breeder, when we mentioned the holes in the lawn. We were totally unprepared for how our new Airedale puppy would turn our lives upside down. Every waking moment was a frenzy of activity and play, such that we took it in turns to retreat for half an hour's peace. To stay and read would mean Airedale-shaped holes in the newspaper.

Things soon settled down, and we all found a way of living together. Digger goes everywhere with us – on days out, weekends away and holidays in the motorhome – and loves all the admirers. We are very disappointed if we don't hear at least once a day, 'Oh look, an Airedale – you don't see many of them nowadays', and then listen to tales of childhoods spent with one, or with grandparents who owned one. All agree that Airedales are great characters and have a mind of their own.

Digger's encounter with the fire-breathing dragon in the sky has been his biggest adventure so far. So terrified was he of the sudden appearance of the low-flying hot-air balloon that in his blind panic to run home he created a new record, and in the process wore away the pads on both back feet. The poor fellow was hobbling around for days afterwards, and since then everything scary comes from the sky.

LIKES sausages and snoozing
DISLIKES water
FINEST HOUR that 'just groomed' handsome Airedale look

Elaine and Gavin Walkingshaw, Wiltshire

Rio, Spanish pure-bred, fearer of noises

R IO IS no Trigger. He is never going to race across inhospitable terrain to pull me from the jaws of death, after which we ride into the sunset with Prefab Sprout's 'Cowboy Dreams' playing in the background.

Rio, or to give him his posh name, Corsario XIII, isn't the

world's bravest horse. Then again, he doesn't have the world's bravest rider – 'what's in the brain, goes down the rein' – and he takes his confidence from me. But into the second year of our partnership, we are learning to trust each other.

Since they were domesticated about 5,000 years ago, the power and intuition of horses have given them a singular place in the lives of men and women. Our earliest encounters may have been with the relatively tiny animals of the Eurasian Steppes, but thousands of years of evolution have given me Rio – and the thought makes me an incredibly happy horse owner.

He is sixteen hands high, seven years old (although his birthday isn't until September, all horses are aged by their birth year, and so on January the first he became seven), and is pure-bred Spanish (also known as PRE or Pura Raza Española).

Crucially, he doesn't have a nasty bone in his body. He is, as they say in horsey circles, 'genuine'. He has a kind eye and willing nature, and always inspires admiring comment. He is quick to learn and will, in time, be as brave as I need him to be. The PRE, after all, was bred for courage – they have been fighting wars, and bulls, for hundreds of years. I think I'll wait a while, though, before I take him into the local field of Friesians.

LIKES he's highly unoriginal: he will do almost anything for apples
DISLIKES anything producing a sudden noise – makes hacks interesting
FINEST HOUR watch this space. He's going to go far, but he'll need a tad more training to get there

Fiona Matthias, Warlingham, Surrey

Henry, big softie

Oᴜʀ Gʀᴇᴀᴛ Dane, Henry, was just eight weeks old when I first saw him, and it was instant love. He has the most wonderful temperament: gentle, laid-back and loving.

It is unusual to hear him bark. This only happens on occasion, such as when we leave him outside for longer than five minutes. His bark is deep and rich, but after a minute or so it breaks, and he sounds all wimpy and pathetic.

As with lots of big dogs, Henry doesn't realize that he weighs almost seventy kilograms. He thinks he is a little thing, and sits himself firmly on my lap at every opportunity. He loves to have the inside of his leg rubbed, and when he is on my lap and I am giving him a gentle scratch, he starts to fall asleep. His breathing changes and his cheeks puff out and in again, his body starts to rock as he falls deeper into sleep, and then we have to be ready to catch him as he falls off.

35

He rolls on his back to have a tickle, which looks very odd as his huge chest dominates his frame and his long legs stick up in the air. His mouth falls back, all gummy, and if he could speak he would say, 'Come on, Mummy, get down here and give me kisses.' He loves to have his armpits rubbed, which are always warm and sweaty.

He has a huge amount of toys. Some are so small they used to be on a key ring – soft padded teddies. Others, like his ball and his hippo, he has had for years. I have never had to stitch anything as he is so gentle.

He doesn't like being told off, and will chatter his teeth just to get some sympathy or attention.

Our walls have stains on them from where he has shaken his head and let loose big blobs of glue-like spit. Even our lovely pictures have spit marks. But this is a small price to pay for the abundance of love and kisses we get every day.

LIKES lots of love
DISLIKES loud noises
FINEST HOUR asleep on his new bed

Berni Albrighton, Warwickshire

Ted, the lion from Oz

TED HAD been living rough before he came to us, and needed his tangled fur clipped off. We decided that he was like the lion in *The Wizard of Oz*, so gentle, timid and nervous. Our fifteen-year-old cat would box his ears if Ted got too close.

In July, we returned from a holiday to find my neighbour, with whom we have a reciprocal cat-feeding arrangement, very upset. Ted had been missing for five days. She had searched, but to no avail. Distraught, I put up notices. Twenty-four hours later, we got a phone call.

Ted was stuck at the top of a tall, straight tree. When I called him, he miaowed pitifully, but would not move. The owner fetched his extendable ladder and climbed up, but Ted was frightened and moved to a thin branch where he could not be reached.

And so I, a seventy-two-year-old grandma with a knee replacement, who hates heights, climbed the ladder. I kept saying to myself, 'Don't look down!' On reaching the top, I talked to Ted, who was miaowing in terror, and he wobbled along the bending branch towards me. He was still on the other side of the trunk. I could reach over and stroke his head, but he was too heavy for me to lift with one hand. I was desperate, and suddenly Ted appeared to be trying to reach me, but slipped. As I put out my hand, he fell towards me and hung on with his paws around my body like a child. I held him and the ladder rungs and very slowly descended. My legs were like jelly, but I managed to put terrified Ted into a basket.

It took Ted about a week to recover, and we think he must have been stuck up the tree almost a week. Hopefully he has eight lives left, but I'm not so sure about myself after that episode. But the love I get from Ted makes it all worthwhile.

LIKES being stroked, treats
DISLIKES visitors, sudden noises
FINEST HOUR hanging on to me, without scratching, on the ladder

Elizabeth Theo, Surrey

Molly, lurcher/greyhound/ Labrador cross

MOLLY WAS unwanted, and had been taken to the Warrington Dogs' Home, Cheshire, in 2008, where we were introduced to her. She was three years old, and we were most impressed with her elegance and quiet demeanour. She was sleek, black, long-legged and beautiful. We found ourselves signing all the documents there and then. We didn't even have a collar and lead for her.

Owning Molly has been an adventure. She is terrified of other dogs, feathers, snowflakes and shadows. The early days saw us frantically searching for her when she slipped her collar after being scared by a sudden noise. We were so worried about losing her, we kept her on a lead on all walks.

One day we took her to a small park. It was fenced and gated and we decided to let her off the lead. Then we took a tennis racket and lobbed a ball across the grass for her. As soon as she saw it, the greyhound in her emerged and she chased after it like there was no tomorrow. It was a sight to behold. It was fantastic to see how those strong back legs could propel her through the air in magnificent leaps to catch the ball in mid-flight. Since then, we have let her off the lead in safe places. When running, she becomes full of confidence. I think this was a turning point, and she is now much happier.

Molly, now seven, is gentle, loving, loyal, intelligent, polite and patient. Her nervousness remains but does not dominate, as in the past. We love her to bits – the best impulse-buy in the world.

LIKES running, sleeping
DISLIKES the dreaded vacuum cleaner
FINEST HOUR Molly didn't bark for the first three months, and when she finally managed it, it was a pathetic, strangled croak. Eventually she got the hang of it, and now her bark is healthy and strong – she saves it for special occasions, like when the delivery man knocks

The Honeyford family, Glossop

Mr Darcy, shy ladies' man

H E ARRIVED with aplomb. Young, beautiful and magnificent, he strutted around our garden with suspicion, wondering if it would compare favourably with his previous home, as his black, brown and white feathers glistened in the sunshine.

Dorothy, Doris, Dusty and Daphne watched from under the rosemary bush as he pecked and scratched as real men do.

At last, he spied the ladies. He seemed to quiver and shake, as if suddenly unsure that he could deal with the advancing army of liberated, self-sufficient females approaching purposefully.

Dorothy, the head in the pecking order, made the first move by flying towards him in what appeared to be an attack. The others followed, but Mr Darcy nimbly sidestepped them and resumed his inspection.

As it grew dark, we watched nervously. The ladies retired first, and Mr Darcy followed. We passed a restless night.

Morning dawned, and we were relieved to see that he was still in one piece – as were his companions. Having heard how demanding a cockerel could be, we feared feathers would be flying. However, Mr Darcy allowed a respectable week or two before expressing his manhood, which from that moment on he did non-stop – and with gusto.

In the end, he couldn't stay. He crowed night and day until our poor neighbours were exhausted. Off he went to a farm, where he lives to this day in the company of other fowl, goats and pigs.

Our ladies are also happy with the new arrangement, as they now have no demands on their time other than laying. We still visit Mr Darcy. When we call him, he turns swiftly, giving us a wink and a loud cock-a-doodle-doo of recognition.

LIKES ladies
DISLIKES being chased
FINEST HOUR becoming a full-blooded male

Liz Lee, Wiltshire

Smudge

OUR FIRST encounter with Smudge wasn't reassuring. She lapped the room of her top-floor tower-block home so fast that her owners had to give us a photograph so we could see what she looked like.

The idea was that Smudge would ease our grief for Galore, our recently deceased and much-loved ginger veteran, whose purring, posing and crowd-pleasing had made her a legend in the area.

But over the next two weeks at home with us, the only proof we had that we owned a cat was the vanishing of food from her bowl and the sounds of top-shelf china crashing to the floor.

Then, one evening, a triangular face peered out at me. She advanced, allowed herself to be stroked and then, out of the blue, fell on her side like a toppled tree. I thought she had expired. Then I felt, rather than heard, the sound of a low purr, like a car engine rusty through disuse. I stroked her stomach, and she stuck four limbs in the air and closed her eyes in ecstasy.

Six months on, and Smudge has taken on much of the mantle of her predecessor. She spends a lot of her time outside, sleeping in the compost heap. She eats the dog's food and climbs on worktops to birdwatch. She will always be somewhat special. Her miaow took weeks to emerge. Toy mice remain a source of terror.

And faced with the unknown, she runs first, asks questions later.

But as she lies by the fire and continues to express her pleasure by falling over, unexpectedly, and with an audible thud, she's now a visible presence, not replacing our old pet but carving her own space in our home and hearts.

LIKES using the coal scuttle instead of the litter tray
DISLIKES anything that comes between her and her food
FINEST HOUR waiting until we were eating Chinese food, catching her own takeaway mouse and crunching it loudly under the table

Charlotte Philips, Surrey

Robert the Bruce

I FIRST met Bob, named after Robert the Bruce, in the summer of 1989. He was starved and weak and terrified of people.

I watched as he hooked meat onto a claw, then lifted it to his nostrils – real food. It took several visits to the vet, during which he showed amazing trust and patience, to heal all his injuries and ailments.

He looked like a wild cat, and had lived like one for some time. At first he bit and scratched, so I was fearful when my younger daughter took to carrying him about, head and paws over her shoulder.

Sometimes her hands slipped to his rear legs as she lifted him – he was as long as she was tall – leaving him dangling, nose millimetres off the floor. Tolerating it all with amazing forbearance, he'd look up at me with a dreamy look as he was parcelled up. He never hurt her.

During one summer, as Bob sat Egyptian-style on my son's knees, a lime-green dragonfly entered the garden, jinking ever closer until it was just centimetres away, eyeball to eyeball with Bob.

We watched, breathless, as he lifted a tentative paw, then lunged at the insect.

There was a sound like a toffee being unwrapped as claws raked through gossamer wing. The dragonfly, apparently unharmed, wobbled briefly closer to Bob's nose, then darted away.

Emerging from the spell, Bob looked around at us, and we all burst into laughter.

On my conscience always will be the months when I saw him but assumed he belonged to someone, and let him go unfed. He was a special and beautiful animal, and a great friend.

LIKES sleeping on his back on the sofa, legs akimbo, an Orlando-like smile on his face
DISLIKES postmen and dustmen
FINEST HOUR firmly standing his ground, regardless, when challenged by hostile cats

David Pope, London NW11

Misty, lurcher

I<small>T WAS</small> a damp, foggy day when we arrived at the RSPCA kennels with our firstborn (our Border collie, Megan) to choose a companion for her, having decided (well, I had decided, with my husband's reluctant agreement) that we had room in our hearts, and in our home, for a second dog.

Down the lines of kennels we tramped, to the accompanying barks and whines of the occupants. On reaching the last kennel – with apparently no one at home – we turned. Suddenly, out of the gloom, a thin, bedraggled lurcher silently appeared, tail wagging slowly like a metronome, while she solemnly eyed us up. *These two might do.*

Full of latent mistrust, Misty the lurcher joined our family. Megan swung from absolute hatred to complete indifference about her, growling ferociously when it was obvious that not only had she been in our car, but she was also coming into her house!

Five years on, the two dogs live in harmony and the sad, frightened little Lurcher has become queen of the settee and all available comfy surfaces. She has learnt how to enjoy life and to trust: no longer does she flinch when we pick up a stick to throw for Megan, but she is still reluctant to pass a suspicious object left in the hall – or the hoover, not in its rightful position.

Neither the postman delivering nor the doorbell ringing have any impact on this most placid of dogs, but occasionally, if Megan's barking is persistent enough, she will rouse herself from her horizontal position to stroll out as 'back-up'. She gives us serenity in our busy lives, and pleasure in abundance.

> **LIKES** cheese, lying on the settee and giving herself a pedicure
> **DISLIKES** being forced to go out in the rain, baths
> **FINEST HOUR** bolting up Yarmouth high street and bringing traffic to a standstill

Julie Stone, King's Lynn

PART THREE

ODD COUPLES AND DEVOTED PAIRINGS

Bess and Frank, old married couple

WE WERE off on a break in Devon. While having coffee, we saw a lady pass the window with a beautiful dog. Out went my husband to find out what it was: an Italian Spinone. We knew we had to have one.

Back home, we rang the Spinone club secretary, only to find there was not one to be had, as selective and careful breeding is so important. But she took our name and phone number.

Life went on. Retirement had no routine, and we were desperate to have a dog and walk the mountains. So along came Bess, a wonderful little black Lab. She quickly became part of our home, as Labs do.

Three years later, the phone rang. There was a fourteen-month-old Spinone available. There were exchanges of letters, pictures and questions: did we have another dog? Did we have space? Did we realize what having a Spinone entailed? The answers were yes, yes and yes. We arranged a meeting point. A car pulled up, and out stepped the most handsome, enormous hulk called Frank.

He has filled our lives with his gentle nature, and loves company. And Bess? Well, she took his toys, took his food and slept in his bed. But Frank let her, and moved his bed to be near her.

Then Frank developed a nasty ear infection. Eventually, he had to have both ear canals removed. He was left deaf, with a slight facial paralysis, and has had to adjust to a world of signs and vibrations. So have we. The paralysis means he takes a long time to eat, so he keeps his head down in the dish and eats outside.

Bess has come to the rescue. She is Frank's ears, and they are inseparable. With her help, Frank functions fine, and barks for her if she is ever out of sight. To quote our kennel-owner friend, 'They are just like an old married couple.'

LIKES pulling apples off the tree
DISLIKES a facial after food
FINEST HOUR recovering, after two operations, into a silent world

Anne Evans

Neville the Feline Pacifist

M Y HUSBAND and I have been married for fifty-two years, and we have had many feline friends in that time. All have had their own personalities, but we have never had a cat as laid-back as Neville.

Neville is so benign that nothing bothers him. Everyone is his friend – or at least, he thinks they are. A complete pacifist, he has never been known to kill or injure anything in his life. Once another cat brought a mouse in alive, and the mouse escaped and ran all over Neville. He never even moved. Neville could even make friends with birds.

We used to open our garden to the public. As soon as the first visitors arrived, he would appear and follow them around. Some attempted to ignore him; he would respond by lying down on the plants to get their attention.

Unfortunately, his advancing years have brought with them feline dementia. He now gets lost around the house, and becomes very distressed when he cannot find us. But with enough love and care, we hope he will be with us for a long while yet.

LIKES smelling the flowers
DISLIKES the rustle of plastic bags
FINEST HOUR that is still to come

Brenda Stuckey, Exmouth

Betty and Timmy

BETTY WAS one of a clutch of bantam eggs hatched by one of our hens, but she was always an individual. Right from the beginning she did her own thing – she'd wander off on her own, or come into the house and sit on the table. Later, when night fell, she would fly up to the top of the broom cupboard to roost, and then fly down again for breakfast in the morning. She retained this individualistic streak all her life. We had a dachshund, Timmy, who was very fond of her and would present her with a bone every now and then for her to peck.

One day, we returned from a country walk to find a fire

engine outside our house. An electrical fault had caused a fire. Luckily it wasn't too serious, but we could not find Betty anywhere and we were worried about her. Suddenly, Timmy started barking excitedly out in the garden. We went outside and found poor Betty hiding in the hedge. She was quite shaken but unhurt, much to everyone's relief, including Timmy, who had saved the day.

As the years went by, Betty got less adventurous. At the age of fourteen, she saw what she thought was a friend at the bottom of the pond. She decided to join the friend, but unfortunately it was only her reflection. Sadly, she was found floating in the pond the next morning. She was dreadfully missed by us all, especially her ally, Timmy.

> **LIKED** joining in meals at the table
> **DISLIKED** being treated as a chicken; she was convinced she was one of us
> **FINEST HOUR** when she laid her first egg

Pauline Peach, West Sussex

Cass and Gnome

S HE WOULDN'T be here if it weren't for my husband, who, in spite of me whispering, 'I don't want a poodle', said into the phone: 'We'll come and see them this afternoon.'

We came home with a blue merle seven-week-old Coldoodle (collie/poodle), and we have never looked back. Cass has everything you could want in a pet: loyalty, obedience, intelligence and an eagerness to please. I have taught her all the usual commands and manners, and she has taught me all I know about her, so that I was able to encourage her interests.

She wasn't keen on the arrival of a small Jack Russell puppy, who we named Gnome, and stared out of the car window not looking at him. But by the time we arrived home, on a windy day, she had tolerated him long enough for us to take a photo of them together before she showed him around his new home. After this, Gnome would take refuge in her bed whenever he felt lonely. Once he found his paws, she allowed him to boss her around, and looked at me as if to say: 'What is it with terriers?'

Cass loved to spend an hour or two watching for the earth to move on a molehill, her head going from side to side with anticipation, waiting to pounce on an unsuspecting mole. She has been successful twice. Being a collie, she was eager to help with sheep, but one day, knowing there was an electric fence between us, I told her to 'stay'. However, so convinced was she that the sheep I had gone to rescue was going to harm me, she came to my aid. In doing so she got caught up in the electric fence, which caused her to take off as fast and as far as she could. My husband drove slowly around our village looking for her, and discovered her cowering in the corner of a field. On calling her, she ran thankfully into his arms. To this day she doesn't like sheep!

These events are memories for Cass now as she approaches her sixteenth birthday, when she will enjoy her customary mini-pork pie, but I want to pay tribute to her qualities and the joy she has given us. I'm so pleased my husband answered that phone!

LIKES pork pies
DISLIKES sheep
FINEST HOUR taking Gnome, our small Jack Russell, under her wing

Rosemary Hart, Norfolk

✳ ✳ ✳

Raf and Coco, flopsy bunnies

I FIRST stumbled upon the idea of having a house bunny when a friend told me what fantastic pets they make if you work full-time: they tend to snooze when you're out and wake up to play when you get home. When she added that they can be easily litter-trained, like cats, and how clean and inquisitive they are, I was sold.

I first met Raf, an extremely fluffy cinnamon-and-white mini-lop bunny, when he was eight weeks old and about the size and colour of a jacket potato. Of all the baby bunnies I saw, he had the most personality, indiscriminately hopping over the heads of the other babies to get my attention, like a tiny kangaroo.

As he grew up, Raf turned out to be quite a character, tugging on my duvet in the morning to wake me up, headbutting my feet when I was on the phone, guarding the fridge at all times and thumping his back foot on the floor if anyone dared to wake him. However, I travel abroad a lot with work, and began to worry that Raf would get lonely, so I decided to find him a friend. I didn't want to go to a breeder again, as I'd since discovered that thousands of bunnies are abandoned or set free every year.

That's when I discovered Greenwich Rabbit Rescue (greenwichrabbitrescue.com), which takes in unwanted rabbits with a view to rehoming them. So last December I took Raf 'bunny-dating'. After a few tricky encounters, he took an immediate shine to Coco, a beautiful, elegant chocolate-brown bunny, who is so happy to be stroked that she squeaks, purrs and carefully places her little paws in your hand to thank you.

Luckily she was also very patient with Raf, who was overexcited about the prospect of a girlfriend. They had both been neutered, and they took about six weeks to bond, but now they couldn't be happier. They insist on doing everything together, cuddle up at every opportunity, sit on the sofa to watch television, navigate the wilds of the garden like lop-eared explorers and have lots of nose-wiggling conversations that I wish I could understand. In short, they're the perfect pets.

LIKES parsley, green beans, dandelions
DISLIKES being woken up
FINEST HOUR collectively breaking into the fridge to steal an Easter egg

Emma Pomfret, London

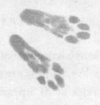

Lamby and William

Lamby should not have survived. A poor little weakling, she was rejected by her mother at birth in favour of her larger, healthier sister. Lamby was left without any motherly protection from predatory foxes, and her fate was in the balance. But my grown-up daughter, Juliet, couldn't bear to see her die.

With permission, Juliet removed Lamby from the farmer's field and ensconced her in the shed in the garden. She let her out to frolic during the day, and fed her at regular intervals. At the same time, Juliet was busy feeding her new baby, William, who had arrived a few weeks before.

Lamby gradually grew stronger, and considered herself an important member of the family. She did not take much notice of our dog and two cats, but relished playing with little William as he got bigger. Never wanting to miss out, she used to poke her head through the cat flap to see if anybody was about. She would sneak into the kitchen at the slightest opportunity, and was in like a flash as soon as the door opened.

Having put on weight, and now able to cope on her own, the

time came for Lamby to go back to the field. Not a good idea, as far as she was concerned! Every time Juliet came to visit, up she would rush to greet her. She would be very put out when it was time for Juliet to leave, and once even squeezed under the fence to follow her home.

Now Lamby herself is a mother of twins. One was healthy, but the other was small and weak. So for Juliet, it was back to square one! Lamby Two is now on the bottle at regular intervals. But this year, there is no new baby. At least, not yet.

LIKES eating out of your hand
DISLIKES being left
FINEST HOUR jumping into the back of the car with Bryher, the dog

Joanna Owens, Hertfordshire

Meg and her flock

LIAISONS WE acquire, or actively seek, can have a profound impact on our lives. Over these past years, the relationship between our Border collie Meg and her 'flock' grew to a depth that was fascinating to witness.

Her flock consisted of more than just ducks; there were also moorhens, two geese and a swan. All of these trusted her, and seemed to recognize the role she played as their protector and guard. Meg, in turn, maintained her ability to herd them together into a tight group, understanding the theory of safety in numbers.

It was also clear that the flock understood this game and, from time to time, ensured Meg knew she could only herd them this way because they allowed her to do it. Of course, these indignant protests were noisy posturing only, designed not to be taken too seriously.

The relationship came to an end when Meg died at the end of October following a short illness. It was a harrowing day, since there had been a rapid decline in her last days, and we struggled to keep her calm in the final hours.

Meg has added another dimension to the people we are – and so has her flock. She was my best friend, in the sense that she became the guardian of all my secrets, and I miss that privilege.

I had thought my relationship with her was the closest it could be. But now I understand the quality of the relationships she had with others, too. Over Meg's last hours, the swan came up to the house and sat on the step by the back door making her familiar throaty sounds every few minutes.

On the other side of the door, in her basket, Meg was listening and acknowledging each sound. When Meg died, the swan remained and kept a vigil for the rest of the day until we buried Meg on the island [in the duck pond] in the late afternoon.

Their liaison clearly went beyond human sentiments and understanding; it had a simplicity and an accepting nature we ourselves would do well to embrace.

LIKES watching the ducks
DISLIKES fireworks
FINEST HOUR her winter ascent of Helvellyn

Sue Fletcher, Staffordshire

PART FOUR

ESCAPE ARTISTS

Daisy, reformed character

DAISY WAS always going to be a rebel. My husband David once rescued her from the road where she was prancing about surrounded by motorbikes taking part in a rally. The riders were all swerving around her and laughing as she chased their wheels.

Once, she escaped and got into the school playground and chased the screaming children round, trying to persuade them to play, while the headmaster looked thunderous and David, pink and puffing, tore after her, shouting commands that were totally ignored.

Another time she dashed into the churchyard, and in her

excitement upended the elderly gardener and his wife who were weeding the path – the wife ending up on her back showing her knickers.

The first time Daisy was in season, she became obsessed with finding freedom and love. She jumped out of the back window of our car one dark winter's night in the middle of town, and then dodged and danced around the street holding up all the traffic.

She was also a terrible thief. She ate a whole Christmas cake and then was horribly sick down the sofa, and she pulled over the Christmas tree, smashing all the baubles, because she had spotted a chocolate decoration right at the top. She also stole a whole box of liqueur chocolates, box, wrapping and all, and greeted our return with a dreamy, squiffy gaze.

She was basically a disaster. One day she broke my nose when she came hurtling in from the garden at full speed and jumped up while I was hoovering the floor.

And then we discovered agility classes. I always say that agility work was the only thing Daisy could really do right. She was so good at it, and clearly loved it. It channelled her energy, and she cottoned on to most obstacles straight away. Eventually she won events at the local club. I will never forget the day she came home with me with two rosettes and a cup. She sat on the patio and looked so proud.

One evening when she was seven years old, Daisy came into my study shivering and in pain. The vet diagnosed a huge tumour on her liver and she was put to sleep the next day. I cried buckets. I miss the cuddles on the sofa, and the withering sideways looks when she was told off.

We still find white hairs everywhere. She is still with us.

LIKES food, agility classes

DISLIKES being told off

FINEST HOUR trying to seduce an elderly Labrador she met in the fields – the owner became one of my best friends

Lynne Hedworth, Bradstock

Madcap Martha

MARTHA, A tortoiseshell-and-white kitten, arrived in our home with Rufus, a ginger tom, and Lucy, a tabby, at eight weeks old, from Cats Protection. Two days later, she went missing. After a frantic search she was found in the back of the tumble dryer, having crawled up the exit hot-air tube and got stuck. It was impossible to get the back off, so we wrenched off the tube and with a 'breech delivery', I managed to pull her out.

Then, just before last Christmas, we were having some work done in a bathroom, which involved removing the side of the bath. We had the foresight to stuff the hole where the pipes went under the floor.

But one evening Martha failed to appear for supper and, putting my ear to the floor, I could hear a faint mewing. Every two hours I called, in the hope she would come out. In the morning, we rang the fire brigade. Six strong firemen appeared, to the surprise of the neighbours, with saws and crowbars.

Their heat-seeking camera found Martha between the bathroom and a bedroom. Out came the furniture, up came the carpet and a hole was cut in the floorboards, but there was a joist between her and the hole. Then a shout: 'She's gone!' No image on the camera. There is a void behind the lavatory, which goes through to the room below. We rushed downstairs, and there was an image on the camera again. Minutes later, with careful use of a small saw, there she was, curled around the soil pipe.

Later, after a meal and a good sleep, she was none the worse for her adventure. It is hoped that these things don't happen in threes. Fortunately, her brother and sister do not have mad ideas!

LIKES small spaces, hunting, fuss, lying in front of the fire
DISLIKES laps, strangers
FINEST HOUR being released from under the floor

Sheila Bradbury

Patty, roamer

A DEAR friend rescues dogs, but she could not deal with a Parson Jack Russell terrier that she had homed. Patty, a pet-shop dog, was found stray on the streets of Salford and is a roamer. She runs off and has, in the past, attacked cats, dogs, horses and anyone in a high-visibility jacket. She was going to be put down.

I offered to help. This meant bringing her into our home, with a major stumbling block being that my wife, while a hardened forensic scientist, has been dog-phobic since she was bitten as a child. We talked, and I finally persuaded her that Patty was just like some dysfunctional teenager in need of an animal Asbo and strict boot camp. If she came to us, she would not be allowed in the house. Max, our son, and I would do all the walks and any dog-poo bagging and, if these conditions were met, maybe we could try for at least three months to change her madness.

So Patty came to live with me and my family. The first few

weeks with her were a real learning curve for us all. However, almost all the village neighbours and friends cheered us on from Sue, the postmistress, to Terry, the pet-friendly postman.

After three months Patty was brought inside our home. She even sat on my knee and, after initial dog-phobic frowns, my wife wanted Patty on her knee too. Max enjoyed knee sessions, but we were afraid of making her form an attachment that would then see her stressed during separation periods. She was made to lie down and relax in her dog tent. Only the occasional surprise noise or knock on the door made her jump into action.

A year on, and we have decided that Patty is definitely one of the best rewards to come out of a challenging year. My wife, once dedicatedly dog-phobic, is now completely cured and adores Patty, her first family companion dog. Max got his wish for a living dog instead of relying on Spot, a soft toy he cuddled from his earliest infant months.

LIKES tripe sticks being hidden in the garden for her to find
DISLIKES rats
FINEST HOUR catching one of twenty rats in one year, and beating Max and his friend at football (she can dribble a ball for England)

Dr David Sands, Heapey Chorley, Lancashire

Clarissa the tortoise, a Houdini

IN 1976, I went to a local pet shop and bought a tortoise. I remember that they charged me the princely sum of £2.50. I called her Clarissa, and soon she became a valued member of the family.

Originally I did not bother with a cage, which caused a lot of tortoise-hunts in our large garden bushes. One evening she could not be found, and had to spend the night outdoors. Luckily, she was back the next day.

However, in July 1989 she went missing completely. During this period I was very worried, and couldn't eat or sleep properly. It seemed to go on for ever.

Finally, eight weeks later, a local man was blackberry-picking and came across 'a stone that moved'. It was Clarissa, and he managed to return her completely unharmed.

Clarissa hibernates each year in a big box of straw. One year, the box was on a high shelf in the garage. When I went in the spring to see if she was awake, I found her at the door of the garage! I have no idea how she escaped from the box, let alone how she got down to the ground. I was just thankful she was OK, and hadn't been run over by the car.

It is twenty-three years now since her escape, so every day is precious. Every year, when she comes out of hibernation alive, it's a relief. She's also a living calendar for winter and spring. All in all, Clarissa is the best £2.50 I ever spent.

LIKES bread and jam
DISLIKES loud noises
FINEST HOUR surviving her various adventures in the wild

Karen Broadhead, Bedfordshire

Charlie, corn snake

FOR MY son Henry's last birthday, after much nagging, we bought him a corn snake. It was not an unparalleled success. Corn snakes (our one, anyway) are a unique combination of boring and scary. Boring because it just slept all day, and scary because whenever you did try to handle it (as per instructions), it would rear up and strike. Tiny as it was, it was most unpleasant and unendearing, like trying to bond with a very angry pencil.

We had a lot of eleven-year-old boys come to see the snake, only nobody ever could because it was always hiding. Henry was too terrified and repulsed to get it out; instead it always had to be my poor husband – equally repulsed but better at hiding it. Henry's three sisters all thought it was disgusting – not helped by the fact that I now kept a tub of dead baby mice in the freezer.

About four months ago, Henry had a big sleepover in his room and everyone wanted to see the snake. We got it out, we put it back, and everyone went to bed.

It was the following morning that we realized the tank hadn't been quite closed and Charlie had, of course, escaped. An entirely fruitless search followed, made harder by the fact that it had to be conducted in the utmost secrecy. If his sisters knew the snake had escaped, complete hysteria would ensue. We have not yet found Charlie, Henry is sworn to secrecy and I have averted suspicion by continuing to feed an empty tank. I expect he's living happily somewhere under our floorboards, growing to some fantastic size eating spiders and drinking from our leaky shower, and one day when he's big enough he will come out and eat his replacement, a much-loved Russian hamster called Isobel.

LIKES being left alone
DISLIKES our family
FINEST HOUR escaping from his tank

Pascale Smets, Blackheath

Callum, bolter

A S A CHILD, I wanted to marry Roy Rogers – because I wanted his horse, Trigger. Sadly, I never managed it. Instead, I bought Callum as my early-retirement present. When I asked the seller if he would suit a novice rider, I should have noticed the slight pause before she said, 'I'm sure he would.' I didn't, and so began fifteen years of being owned by a shifty, selfish, stunning horse.

Callum has, in general, a very benign temperament. People say you should never give a horse titbits because it makes them nip. Callum has had plenty of titbits since day one, and has never nipped. He is completely trustworthy with dogs and children. I have taught him to give me a kiss for a carrot and to say 'please' by lifting a front leg. He tolerates affection, but finds it unnecessary. Point a camera at him, however, and he'll pose all day.

I don't ride him as much as sit on him and pray. Callum is exceptionally intelligent. Like all horses, he can have shifty days when he pretends to be frightened of something quite ordinary, just to see if he can worry me. Mostly he succeeds. To celebrate his twenty-first birthday, he bucked me off and put me on crutches for two weeks.

Bath day is a battle of wills. He pretends to be frightened of the hose. He ends up looking clean and beautiful; I look like I've fallen in a pool.

One day he saw that the main yard gate was open. He broke loose and started towards it. As he passed me, in a futile attempt to halt him I grabbed his tail. Luckily, only cows were around to see me towed up the lane at a trot.

LIKES Clarnico peppermint creams and carrots
DISLIKES going in a horsebox
FINEST HOUR standing still and waiting for me to mount bareback from a chair. After several attempts, I went straight over his back and landed on the other side

Sue Ajax-Lewis, West Sussex

Buster, the missing cat

O NE DAY, Buster went missing. As the days turned into weeks and months, I began to wonder if we would ever see him again. I put posters up around our area, went from door to door asking if anyone had seen him and placed adverts in the local papers. The result of this was that I went on many a wild-goose chase to look at cats that supposedly fitted his description, only to be disappointed when I got there.

A year passed, and we decided to move house. By that time I had accepted that I would probably never see Buster again. Even so, I left a picture of him with the new owner of our flat, urging her to get in contact with us if he ever managed to make his way back.

Later on, I decided to give a home to two rescue cats. Buster was not forgotten, but he certainly went to the back of my mind.

Then the strangest thing happened. I received a phone call from a vet fifteen miles away, telling me they had my cat. I was sure there had been a mistake, as both of them were snoozing on the sofa. But it was Buster. I nearly fell over. It was such a total shock, as I truly thought I'd never see him again. But when I heard his distinctive Siamese voice over the telephone, I knew in my bones that it was him.

It's still very strange to see him lolling on our bed after disappearing for so long, but it is fabulous to have him home with us.

In a final twist, the local paper got hold of Buster's story and we were contacted by the family he had been living with for five years. He had obviously been much loved, as he came back rather chubby.

The family called him 'Big Cat', and they have asked if they could look after him for us if we ever go on holiday. So all's well that ends well.

LIKES playing pinball, hogging armchairs, travelling
DISLIKES his newly acquired siblings
FINEST HOUR catching a snail for the first time, aged four months

Emma Spink, Pembury, Kent

Scratchy, ferret

Tomorrow I am taking our ferret to the vet to discuss his 'quality of life'. I fear an unhappy outcome, as Scratchy was diagnosed with arthritis some weeks ago, and he has little use of his back legs.

Scratchy belonged to my son, who was unable to keep him, so I offered him a home three years ago, thinking that ferrets were vicious, smelly creatures. Smelly, yes – he is an 'entire' male, and I suppose the lady ferrets find it appealing – but vicious, no. He is amusing, inquisitive, acrobatic and affectionate.

He is also a master of escape.

One Easter, he went down the road, over the river and into a primary school's playground. The kindly caretaker recognized that he was a runaway and put him overnight in a vacant guinea-pig cage. He appeared on the town website and word got around, so I was able to retrieve him.

But his latest adventure was his best by far. He went into our neighbour's garden down the road and disappeared. The 'Lost Ferret' posters went up. Two days later I took a picture to the vet and met a man carrying a 'Found Ferret' poster. Scratchy had spent two blissful nights with a pair of very pretty little-girl ferrets in their super-deluxe accommodation, and was reluctant to come home.

Now, sadly, he stays mostly at home reflecting on his glory days.

LIKES adventures, escaping, hiding
DISLIKES being stuck at home, exercising on a harness
FINEST HOUR a rendezvous with two female ferrets

Elizabeth Lyne, Hampshire

Sam, spaniel

IT BEGAN as just another Monday morning, back in November 2007. I was feeding the animals on our farm, the dogs at my side. At a quarter to eight I knew Sam was still with me. Ten minutes later, he was missing. I always carry a dog whistle, but this time Sam didn't return. I wasn't too concerned at first because the farthest he would ever go was up to the country lane. But half an hour had passed, and my husband and I were getting very concerned.

The day came to an end and we were devastated. I had phoned the police, dog warden, Petlog (Sam was microchipped) and numerous vets. It was a wild and rainy night: we knew Sam hated bad weather and would have come home if he could.

Over the next few days the whole community searched. Posters went up; we put an ad in the local paper with a reward for Sam's return. We even contacted an 'animal communicator' who 'located' Sam in a nearby wood – but we found nothing.

After three months, the animal communicator said that Sam had been shot by a farmer for chasing chickens. My husband never believed the story, but for me this meant that any hope had come to an end. We knew we would never see that lovely, friendly ginger dog, with not a bad bone in his body, ever again.

On 14 April 2010 we had a message on our answerphone – a man from a council saying he had Sam. The hour-and-a-half drive seemed like an eternity. We were excited and nervous – what if it wasn't Sam? I walked to the car park, shaking with nerves. And Sam came bounding towards us. We were in tears. He was fat: he'd clearly been looked after. When we got him home he went crazy, wagging his tail. Later that afternoon he brought me a hen's egg gently in his mouth as he always had before, and that night he slept in his old place in the coat cupboard. Sam was reunited with us after his microchip had been scanned – I would urge other pet owners to do the same (go to www.petlog.org.uk).

LIKES carrying hens' eggs
DISLIKES storms
FINEST HOUR being reunited with us

Christine Robinson, Devon

PART FIVE

GREAT SURVIVORS

Poppy, Georgie and Tally

TWO AND a half years ago, our neighbours brought home a black Patterdale terrier and her two puppies. They had found them running along a path by a dual carriageway, and contacted the police.

My partner Paul and I had always dreamed that a rescue dog would find its way to us – and here were three! But it was not to be. As soon as the owner arrived, the mother dog recoiled. He grabbed her and put a lead on. We all felt sick. She was petrified of him. He roughly scooped up the puppies and proceeded out of the house, dragging the mother along.

Halfway through the side gate, my neighbour snapped: 'You're not taking them.' She trapped the owner mid-exit, and tried to wrestle the mother from him. It was getting nasty. I followed him to his car. 'Please stop,' I said. 'We love the dogs. Please, I'll give you money.' He drove off.

Next day, the man phoned and said he'd sell them. The transaction took place in a car park, very High Noon. I gave him the £435 he'd demanded (a small price for three precious lives). The deal was done. I asked: 'When were the puppies born?' The man said: 'September the fourteenth.' That made them even more special. It was my dear sister's birthday. She died of cancer some years ago. She adored dogs. I wondered if she'd had some celestial hand in all this.

LIKES chasing rabbits, toy tugs-of-war, eating chicken
DISLIKES the postman and window cleaners
FINEST HOUR their escape

Megan Aspel, Surrey

Murphy, miracle cat

A T THIRTEEN years old, Murphy – also known as 'The Bear' – is a miracle cat, according to our vet. Born in a rough part of town, he was rescued at eighteen months with nothing to his name but a hernia. And, it transpired, FIV, the feline version of HIV.

Eleven years on, and typically for this particular individual, Murphy has flown in the face of the statistics by living three times longer than the average FIV cat. He is still bouncing around like a two-year-old when he should have been shuffling off the old mortal coil years ago. It's just that nobody told him.

He eats like a horse, plays with the female cat from next door and is the scourge of the local shrew population. At night, his is the sleep of the righteous, as he snores happily in his bed made from my husband's plush (now former) dressing gown.

When we went away and left him in the cattery for the first time, I wailed more than he did – we toasted him that evening. So began a tradition that even our friends and family continue when they come to dinner: 'One for The Bear,' we all chorus.

Some still believe that the best thing for all FIV cats is euthanasia. Perhaps Murphy can persuade them otherwise. After all, if a positive 'cattitude' was something you could bottle and sell, he'd be worth millions. Ladies and gentlemen, please raise your glasses. I give you The Bear!

LIKES buttered toast
DISLIKES hand cream
FINEST HOUR putting the frighteners on two large dogs
by following them up the road, hissing

Annette Bushell, Bristol

Jackson, deer bait

JACKSON FIRST hurtled into my life nine years ago, with a red balloon attached to his collar and the biggest grin you've ever seen, a gift from my children on Mothering Sunday.

Right from the start he was no conventional dachshund; no long silky-smooth coat seen on pedigrees in smart London parks. Rather, he was quite chunky and his coat curly, but with his loving character, he was instantly one of the family.

I have walked my dogs in Richmond Park for almost forty years, and on one hot summer day, we took our usual favourite stroll. Suddenly I heard Jackson scream behind me and in horror turned to see a huge female deer attacking him. My darling dog was on the ground, not moving, whimpering as the deer reared up on hind legs ready to land on him with two hooves.

She towered above me but I screamed, waving my arms, trying to stop another attack. There was no one near to help.

I dashed forward, scooped him up and ran with him, blood pouring, towards the car park. I could not believe it when I heard, behind my shoulder, the deer following me, forcing me to pick up a stick and run backwards, shouting to keep her at bay.

We drove straight to the vet. Jackson had two perfect

hoofprints on his back. The vet said that the outcome did not look good as the internal organs were probably damaged from the pressure of such a massive force. I waited three anxious hours only to be told that he was the luckiest little dachshund, as the organs were undamaged. Soon he was totally back to his old energetic self, chasing our cats as if nothing had happened. It took me longer to recover!

Enough excitement for one dachshund's life, you would think, but three years later we got a call from my brother-in-law, who was looking after Jackson, to say that his back legs had collapsed. He had been taken to a veterinary training college; should they operate?

My husband and I were halfway up Kilimanjaro. We were distraught, but told them to go ahead with the operation. All went well at first, but then Jackson collapsed again – should they put him to sleep?

Luckily, this was a teaching hospital. They discovered a blood clot, which was cleared, and a steel pin was inserted in his spine. It was the first double operation the college had done successfully.

At last I could bring him home, and there followed intensive rehabilitation, including swimming three times a week and massages to strengthen the wasted back-leg muscles.

Jackson has now worked out the best way to move his legs, even though his gait isn't what it was, but his courage and good nature are humbling. How pleased we are that we said yes to that second operation.

LIKES chasing motorbikes, cats
DISLIKES the rain
FINEST HOUR walking unaided for the first time

Angela Cook, London

Aslan, deaf cat

A T THE back end of 2011, I came across the Nine Lives Greece website and saw that there was an all-white deaf cat called Aslan who desperately needed a safe home. After speaking to Cordelia at Nine Lives, we decided that I would go to Greece to meet Aslan, as he had been through so many terrible things – such as having acid thrown over him. In December I arrived in Athens and met with Cordelia and Eleni, who both showed me many of the cat-feeding sites and introduced me to a half calico, half tabby cat called 'Princess' Madge who was also desperately in need of a home. When I met Madge she was so timid, and hid away. As we walked around central Athens, meeting many of the cats, we came across Bobs, a tiny calico that had somehow lost her tail, but danced around the streets rubbing around anyone she could.

A few days later I met Aslan, who was half wild but obsessed with food. After meeting him a few times I finally managed to stroke him, and he had the most beautiful-coloured eyes (one blue and one amber). On the last trip to see Aslan we found a tiny, blind black kitten (Ilios) sat by the roadside, coughing, sneezing and shaking. I picked him up and he immediately wrapped his arms around my neck and we took him to Aslan's house to treat him.

On arriving back in England, we arranged for Aslan, Madge, Bobs and Ilios to come and live with me. In the meantime, two other cats (Rupert, who had passed out in the middle of a road, and Markos, a deaf white cat) also joined the list to come to the UK.

They have been here since March, and have all settled in. Although Ilios is blind, he spends his days whizzing around the house and has an amazing memory for where everything is. Aslan believes that I am his personal servant but lies with his arms wrapped around me all night. Bobs dances everywhere she goes and is dating Markos. Madge is still a princess and has to eat from a crystal bowl. Rupert is responsible for all naughty behaviour, and has an amazing ability to lead the other cats into many ridiculous situations.

If it hadn't been for Aslan needing a home, none of the other cats would be here.

LIKES eating, and sleeping in my arms
DISLIKES meeting anyone who doesn't give him food
FINEST HOUR trusting humans again after being badly treated

Andrew Dean, Stockton-on-Tees

Harriet and Daisy, springer spaniels

Harriet, our springer spaniel, has a curly brown-and-white coat and large soulful eyes, but a nervous disposition. We thought it would be nice for her to have puppies. Initially she rejected all offers, but at the third try she danced around her prospective mate and succumbed. We constructed a whelping box and remained in attendance when she gave birth to three puppies. The large, pleading eyes gazed at us in horror at what was happening. She allowed the larger, fatter female to suckle, but rejected the tiny female, who we called Daisy.

I decided to try to save Daisy, even though she only fitted into my palm. I bought puppy milk and fed her every four hours with a dropper. She was very weak, but lapped at the milk. The next day, I left for work leaving her wrapped in a warm towel in a safe place. She lay inert, but when I returned she was still breathing. I was jubilant. After another twenty-four hours I tried to get her to feed from her mother. Harriet would only let her suckle if I held her while she latched on. I continued to feed Daisy myself and, against all the odds, she survived.

Daisy was a whizz at sniffing out balls hidden on the golf course, our favourite walk. She even saved her mother's life when she fell off a narrowboat on holiday. We fished Harriet out, apparently unhurt, and settled her down for the night, only to be woken later by bloodcurdling howls from Daisy. Her mother lay in a pool of blood, coming from a laceration hidden in her coat. Thankfully, she made an excellent recovery.

LIKES chasing balls and birds
DISLIKES large dogs and gunshots
FINEST HOUR Daisy's warning, and Harriet attending the vet's willingly, following the narrowboat accident

June French, Kent

Henri, French duck

HENRI (SHE should have been called Henrietta, we later discovered) was saved from certain death at the hands of the French when we bought her at a Brittany market while on holiday. She lived with us in our rented cottage until we had to return home. She then lodged with the chickens next door, which belonged to an oyster farmer.

When we had all the legal documents for her international travel, we returned. We escorted her by ferry to England, to take up residence at our farm.

She had to be in quarantine for thirty days, and could not mix with other poultry. But she became friends with one of the chickens through the fence. Sadly, the chicken was dispatched by a fox before they could meet face to face.

As a general rule, Henri decided to live in the garden. During the day, however, she took up residence under the kitchen table, or in the dog's bed. If human or animal got too close, they were promptly pecked until they retreated.

Henri hated the other ducks we introduced to her for company (and who had to live elsewhere). She bossed the dogs around, and even the horses if they were in the same field. She tolerated human company, and if she felt particularly affectionate she would jump on your back and allow herself to be carried back to barracks for the night. She ruled the household for nine years until she succumbed to pneumonia. She never laid an egg, or tried to fly or consort with a drake. Henri was a wonderful duck, and to this day is sorely missed.

LIKES acting as a model for art students
DISLIKES having to act like a duck
FINEST HOUR chasing off a trained police dog

Katy Fletcher

Bonzo, German pointer,
beater of odds

BONZO WAS a tiny, skeletal puppy when he was found outside a village in Northern Cyprus on a sweltering August day eleven years ago. He showed spirit from the first, barking loudly at other dogs, and he had two rows of teeth, giving him a shark-like appearance. With a careful diet of frequent tiny, nourishing meals he began to put on weight, and he had his vaccinations. At a year old he was a healthy, happy dog, about half the size of a normal German pointer. That's when his life was threatened again. One day he discovered a snake, and unfortunately it was an adder, which bit him in the neck. His head swelled up and

88

he went blind. Luckily the vet prescribed the right treatment – he was put on a drip and received various injections including antihistamines. It took three weeks, but at last he recovered, to the enormous relief of the family. He recovered his sight and the wound opened up, leaving a long scar and a sagging appearance to his neck, which he has to this day.

When he was three years old, we decided to return to England to live and we brought seven dogs, including Bonzo, to live in Chipping Norton in the Cotswolds. They soon settled down to English life, and there is nothing Bonzo enjoys more than a nice cup of tea!

He sunbathes in warm weather and wears a woolly jumper when it's cold. In the evenings he lies on the sofa, covered up with his woolly blanket, and snores loudly.

He's a lovely fellow, getting quite an old boy now, but has plenty of energy and enjoys walking in the fields with the other dogs.

LIKES anything to eat
DISLIKES small male dogs
FINEST HOUR having a massage

Jenny Hayward, Chipping Norton

Frodo, blind genius

ORIGINALLY FRODO came, with his brother Bilbo, from the animal shelter to live with my neighbour and her three other cats. Frodo found fitting in with his new family hard. He started to jump over the fence into our garden to seek peace and quiet. He spent more and more time here, and finally wheedled his way into the house. He was put out at night to go home, but would climb onto the roof and scratch on our bedroom window at three in the morning. We eventually let him sleep over.

Last year, I noticed his eyes were cloudy. The vet said that he was completely blind, which was a shock. How long he had been like that I don't know, but he was getting around just fine at home. He had some tests, and is on pills for high blood pressure. I thought he might have to become a house cat, but soon after he was diagnosed I left a window open and he was off, returning soon afterwards. I decided to let him live his life exactly as before, and he copes very well, only bumping into things that have been left out of place.

I sometimes see him on the roof of the house, and my heart

skips a beat when he jumps onto the garage roof, but he knows what he is doing.

He is a truly contented cat, and returns to my neighbour from time to time for a meal.

He is eighteen now, and everything is well in Frodo's world.

LIKES fillet steak, hot-water bottles and the television quiz show The Chase
DISLIKES the same menu two days running
FINEST HOUR finally being accepted into the house

Jane Howard, Cheltenham

Sonya, dachshund

THE FIRST sign of trouble flaring up came when Sonya, one of our two dachshunds, started to lag behind on our walks. Our vet said that she had spinal problems, and prescribed anti-inflammatories and total rest. Things deteriorated over

Christmas. The temperature dropped and the snow came down. One night, Sonya could hardly walk around the garden and she collapsed in the flower bed. On New Year's Eve, she had an emergency operation at a veterinary hospital. There was no certainty of a successful outcome, but we had no option: the surgeon advised that there was no chance of a normal life for Sonya without it.

We heard news of the outcome just before midnight. The operation had gone well, but it was too early to predict whether it would be successful in the long term.

The freezing weather continued: new snow fell on old snow and was over a foot deep in parts. The roads had become more and more difficult to negotiate. Still, we managed to get Sonya home, despite the conditions.

We dug a circular track for her out of the snow in the garden. With a sling under her back legs to provide her with support, she managed the short walk. Slowly she strengthened, and we dug out a longer walk in the snow so that she could totter around a bit more. We were lucky: now she has recovered almost all her former mobility.

The joy it gives us every day to see her walking, running and playing with our other dachshund is almost indescribable, and never will we forget that snow.

LIKES caravan holidays
DISLIKES postmen
FINEST HOUR first day home from the breeder, a four-legged friend to greet her, a large garden to play in and a warm soft bed all to herself

James Dutton, Daventry

Manuka, micro pig

SHE WAS born on 2 January 2010, the smallest of a litter of six piglets, the most beautiful sandy-brown colour and as cute as a button. On the third day of her life something terrible happened: the heat lamp that was keeping them warm in the cold weather fell into the bedding and the hot wire seared through this little piglet's thigh right to the bone.

Although the wound was cauterized by the heat, it was very nasty indeed. She was found cold and limp in the corner of the farrowing shed on our pig farm. She was immediately brought inside, wrapped in a blanket and placed on top of the radiator.

Then the worst happened – she stopped breathing. What to do? Mouth-to-mouth and heart massage started. After about five minutes she began breathing again. Then the intensive care started. Tiny amounts of fluids were fed to her hourly through the night to keep her strength up, and by the morning she was able to stand on all four tiny trotters.

Although she was getting stronger, the wound was serious, so the decision was taken to treat it with manuka honey, as I had heard it had well-documented healing properties.

Over the next five days the piglet continued to improve with round-the-clock three-hourly feeds, and the wound healed completely. The tissue regenerated itself almost before our eyes – it was amazing. My other animals, especially Hector the cat and Daisy Doo the dog, bonded with her, and she used the cat flap to go outside. She developed a cheeky, loving character. Now, nearly a year on, she is an extremely healthy, happy pig. Her name? Manuka, of course!

LIKES belly rubbing
DISLIKES getting up early
FINEST HOUR discovering how to open the crisp cupboard

Jane Croft, Cambridgeshire

Parsley, adventurer

H E WAS about a year old when he came to us, crying outside the back door. We had three other cats, so after a good feed we showed him the door. Four cats was probably one too many, and in any case it looked as if he belonged to somebody else.

The next morning he was back again. He was allowed to stay until we found his true home. A notice in the village brought a family from a couple of miles away, and they took him away; two days later, he was back. The owners were tired of collecting him. The other three cats accepted him, although Rosie, our rescue matriarch, was not entirely happy. She used to box his ears, though Parsley never made a fuss.

He was a grand chap, full of fun and affectionate, too. He loved living with us and his companions in the countryside around. He sometimes came for a walk with us, and managed to get a rabbit through the cat flap on at least two occasions, and once we found a pair of furry 'trousers' underneath the stairs.

It was his adventurous spirit which eventually got him into trouble. After about ten years with us, he disappeared for a long time. I put up a notice in the village. Fifteen days later, a woman rang my bell to say that she thought she had found Parsley. He was 100 yards up the road, underneath a hedge, with a four-pound steel gin trap with a three-inch spike on his right front leg.

Rather than putting him down, the vet had to amputate. Ten days later, he was back again and after a period of recuperation was full of beans and could even cope with the cat flap. I told the police and RSPCA; the local farm was very angry about the trap.

Parsley got slower and slower. Eventually he couldn't get out through the cat flap, so we used to carry him out and put him on the grass in the sunshine. We had to rush out and get him in if it rained. Finally, this year, when he must have been twenty-one, he could not get up after falling over, and we knew the end had come. After giving him a last cuddle, we took him on a one-way trip.

LIKES lying peacefully in the sun
DISLIKES nothing. He was far too cheerful
FINEST HOUR surviving a gin trap (illegal since the fifties)

Richard Statham, Langport, Somerset

PART SIX

JOY GIVERS

Tina, the bear

Tina was a six-month-old orphan bear, her mother having fallen to a poacher, so I offered to adopt her. We bonded with great bear hugs, and she settled happily in my garden in King Albert Park, Singapore, where I lived for four years in the sixties. Tina lived in three trees: her play tree, which she gradually tore to pieces, her siesta tree, for resting after a good lunch, and her night-night tree.

Every morning she descended her tree and came to sit on the wall beneath my bedroom window and barked at me to get up. I came down and sat beside her with my arm around her fat tummy and her arm around me, while she poked her nose and sticky tongue in my right ear and deafened me with her 'I love you' hum.

Next came breakfast; a large dish of fruit and her favourite poached eggs, all spoon-fed to her by my Chinese cook's eleven-year-old daughter. After breakfast, her bath was filled and she revelled in a long wallow, culminating in drinking her bath water, as all well-brought-up bears do.

Then came a walk. She was easier to train than a dog, and would come when called (nearly always), walked at heel, and when walking through long grass got up on her hind legs and held my hand in case anything should suddenly jump out at her.

It was widely known that she liked beer, and after her walks she would often receive gifts, but never became an alcoholic. She doted on honey, a useful bribe, but she discovered that it was kept in the refrigerator. Consequently she tore the door open one day and took both her honey and my next day's meals.

She hated thunderstorms. Seated comfortably in my armchair, I would first hear the storm beginning with heavy rain, then barking and much bustling, and then a thoroughly sodden bear would burst into the room and land heavily on my lap.

I have had many wonderful dogs as pets, but Tina the bear was quite exceptional.

LIKES honey, beer, baths
DISLIKES thunderstorms
FINEST HOUR destroying the fridge

Sir Peter Whiteley, Devon

❊ ❊ ❊

Pixie, West Highland White

IT WAS a note left on the kitchen table that finally won me over. *Dear Daddy, I must have a dog or I will go mad. Love Millie.*

After months of psychological warfare waged by my wife, Jo and daughters, Millie and Eloise, I finally succumbed and, one Saturday in March 2008, Pixie, a West Highland terrier, inveigled her way into the family home, to the evident dismay of our three cats.

Their disdain was equalled only by mine. I had never been a dog lover, and insisted I would have nothing to do with her. My resolve soon faltered, of course. The girls gleefully chronicled my every surrender: covert cuddles; runs in the park.

The first year of Pixie's life was eventful. First, she broke her hip in a mysterious accident on the beach. No sooner had she recovered from intensive weekly physiotherapy (including, I kid you not, sessions on an underwater treadmill), than she was being rushed to the animal hospital after overdosing on Nurofen (the packet had been knocked from a kitchen worktop, so the cats were our chief suspects); a few weeks later, she ran onto a busy main road and was hit by a car.

It's true, she has put up with a lot – I once spotted her wearing a nappy and being wheeled around in a toy pram – but she has an unfailingly sunny personality. And she hasn't been near the vet for months. One mystery remains, though. I had always thought that, for dogs, 'walkies' was nirvana. Not Pixie. She has a stubborn streak. Sit-down strikes, lie-down strikes – we've had them all. Is it a Westie trait? Can other owners enlighten me?

LIKES cuddling up on the sofa, chasing squirrels (and our cats), children

DISLIKES being bathed, healthy organic dog food, exerting herself before mid-morning

FINEST HOUR second prize at the Ham and Petersham Fair dog show

Tim Jotischky, West London

Ludo, Nova Scotia Duck Tolling Retriever

I AM fast asleep when someone shoves a filthy, smelly, wet floor mop in my face. Startled, I open my eyes. And there is Ludo, grinning, two inches from my nose.

Ludo is always happy; he greets each day with enthusiasm, a trait I sometimes find hard to share. Like now. But usually, by the time I have run or, more often, walked around our nearby lake, I feel ready to face the world with my dog's exuberance. Well, almost.

Ludo lives up to his name, which means 'I play', which is odd, because he was only called that because the cat is called Domino. She also lives up to her name, which, more or less, means 'mistress of the house', although her name was obvious because she is white with black spots.

Ludo charms everyone he meets with his trusting eyes, broad beam and waggy tail. People often ask me what his parents were, which is annoying.

He is a Nova Scotia Duck Tolling Retriever: after some slow reiteration, they can sometimes repeat it back. To the initiated, they are just Tollers. Tolling means luring ducks within gunshot range.

Nova Scotia Duck Tolling Retrievers are quite new here, and were only recently recognized by the Kennel Club and allowed to exhibit at Crufts. I think they will take over the doggy world.

Ludo is nine, but still has the bounce and speed of a two-year-old. You can throw sticks all day and he will still ask for more, although he feels it the next day.

But I digress: the filthy mop needs his walk. Perhaps I'll run. You may see us: Ludo is bright orange, so hard to miss – except in autumn, when he is hard to find.

LIKES squeaky toys, balls
DISLIKES being left behind when the pack goes out
FINEST HOUR passing his puppy-training exams with flying colours

Alison Green, Surrey

Dobson, springer spaniel/ red setter cross

DOBSON WAS the most handsome dog in the world, and had a map of India on one side. Although we never knew his exact age, he was born in the autumn, so I gave him an official birthday, like the Queen, on 3 October, the same date as mine. I think he was probably given as a Christmas present, as he would have been ready to leave his mother at that time of year.

He was handed in to the animal shelter during the school holidays when he was about eighteen months old: it was thought he was dumped to avoid the kennel fees while his owners went away.

I think he knew how to behave, but just found it too difficult. He developed a taste for seat belts early on, and managed to chew through many in his lifetime.

Before I had him neutered – which calmed him down a bit – he managed to get at some food placed on the cooker extractor fan. I never understood how he did this, short of getting the folding steps out of the hall cupboard. He also used to eat house flowers during this fraught period, but only the chrysanthemums. He succeeded in extracting them from a tall, thin vase on a windowsill without disturbing the vase or the other flowers in it. Once, he was swimming in the park and picked up a seagull and swam to me with it. I was surprised; the seagull was irate.

I've lost count of the times I have been to the vet with him, with ear infections, seeds in the ears and once with a badly swollen leg after swimming in a stream and being bitten. Then there was the time he had an injury after, I suspected, an altercation with a swan.

He was put to sleep in July after weeks battling cancer. I scattered his ashes in all his favourite places. There never was a creature with such joie de vivre. He will live in my heart for ever.

LIKES water, carrots, life in general
DISLIKES any form of chocolate, the vet
FINEST HOUR sending up a pheasant for the first time from a hedge at close quarters. Also winning four rosettes for doing clear rounds in agility contests

Sandra Hurst, Gloucestershire

Benjy, rescue terrier

BORN IN 2000, Benjy is half Yorkshire terrier and half Jack Russell. He behaves as if he were 100 per cent Jack Russell, but his coat is silky and fine.

Benjy was a year old when we got him, and we were his third set of owners. The first owner was a girl who moved into a flat where no dogs were allowed; the second was a family that neglected him, and who had a Staffy who bullied him.

We saw Benjy advertised in a local pet shop. We were surprised when we walked into the house where he lived: he was confined to a small downstairs room and was under the table, and not allowed into the rest of the house. We fell in love with him immediately. My husband David picked him up and he wouldn't get down. We handed over the money and left. No one even said goodbye to him.

Benjy was sick in the car on the way home, and has been the same ever since. Luckily we discovered a natural spray called Adaptil DAP (Dog Appeasing Pheromone), which you can use in the car before you set off. It has a calming effect, so now he can travel most times with no bother.

Benjy walks miles with David, and is well known in the village. They meet up in the Playskool with ten other dogs and their owners. He has fallen in love with a lady Jack Russell called Megan. She is younger than him and treats him roughly, but he is smitten and he looks for her every day when passing the top of her road. Our grandchildren have grown up with him and he loves them. He will be thirteen next March, is in good health and enjoys life. We can't imagine ever being without him.

LIKES biscuits, walks and Megan
DISLIKES the vet, birds and cats
FINEST HOUR stealing David's ham sandwich the first day in his new home

Mr and Mrs David Harrison, Sittingbourne

Sam, golden retriever

S AM IS fourteen. His pace these days may be described as funeral minus: cars stop in our village to let him pass.

People wind down their car windows and ask, 'How old is she?' He isn't insulted; he takes it all in his stride.

Sam landed on his paws in life. Our daughter found him late one night rooting in bins, and adopted him. He was six months old. No one claimed him in the following weeks. 'Please,' she asked us, 'can you take him on for me?' Nearly fourteen years on, he remains ours. He loved Abbie, our four-year-old retriever, and, since she died, he shares bossing the household with our two Burmese cats.

From the early days he liked to hold his lead in his mouth. We put it down to insecurity. If he had his lead, we figured, he couldn't get lost. He has some other strange habits. Having worked through his car-hating phase and his early escaping fetish, he now loves the car and stays close to home.

A few years ago he entered a phase of digging to Australia. He led other dogs into bad habits; they watched him with interest and suddenly craters appeared everywhere. He has worn out his paws and teeth and developed arthritis. No wonder.

Possessing zero road sense, he once headbutted a car. He'd run ahead of me, and under a gate. When I reached the road, the driver was a nervous wreck. Having exonerated the driver from any blame, I discovered Sam had shot down the road like a missile. For a week or two, he was jumpy when a car accelerated past. It didn't last.

He also brings presents to visitors. Once, he approached us at the door dragging the cat bed with a bewildered cat sitting in it! Another time, we were hosting a renowned male bass soloist. As we opened the front door, returning from a concert, there was Sam, tail wagging, and in his mouth the only 'presents' he could find. Having trawled the house, he had decided upon the visitor's pants and socks, which he proceeded to nudge at his shins until he picked them up. Retriever . . . absolutely!

LIKES any rodent scent that invites digging
DISLIKES having Vaseline put on his nose
FINEST HOUR those pants and socks!

Martin and Sue Winbolt-Lewis, Bramphope, near Otley

Charlie, furball and rescuer

WHEN OUR beloved golden retriever died at the age of thirteen, our lives stopped as well. My wife Jan and I totally lost direction in our retirement, and found endless reasons to do nothing for two years.

On one exceptional occasion, when we visited the coast, we met a man trying to socialize a small dog he'd just got from a rescue centre. We had been considering helping a dog in reduced circumstances, and our chance meeting seemed to be a signal. What followed was a catalogue of fluke occurrences, any one of which would have stopped our progress, but they all fell in our favour. We visited The Dogs Trust in Canterbury and there was Charlie. He'd just been handed in at nine months, and had not been examined, but we were allowed to put our name on the list. A week later he'd been checked over, we'd been checked over and he was permitted to leave with us. It was obvious that the ordeal of being given up had unsettled him, and it was quite a while before he felt that ours was his new home.

Slowly his confidence returned and his true character emerged – and what a character: loving, intelligent, humorous and friendly. Charlie, now two and a half, gets me up at six and follows me into the bathroom where he points to what's next. He anticipates everything, pointing us in the right direction all day. He knows it's Bonio time when he hears the *EastEnders* music, and finishes his day by cuddling up to us on our bed for five minutes before he retires to his own.

Strictly speaking, we rescued Charlie, but in fact, he rescued us. Life has returned to normal. But we still miss our retriever. Like all the other dogs in the neighbourhood, she would have loved Charlie. This photo is used as a wallpaper for our computer to remind us about what's important in life, just in case we lose our way again, although that's not likely with Charlie around.

LIKES stealing slippers
DISLIKES aggressive dogs
FINEST HOUR bringing happiness to everyone he meets

Phil and Jan Horton, Kent

Orla, Labrador cross

As soon as he had acquired the necessary words, my son Edward made it clear that his greatest desire would be to have a dog. It took until he was fifteen for us to feel brave enough to accede to his wishes, and even then my husband had serious reservations about the effect it might have on the cat.

In autumn 2008 we brought home a squirming bundle from a litter of eight. We had chosen Orla for her boldness and energy; traits that left us a little dazed in her first few days at home. However, Edward was always there to show her love, and she soon began to work her charm on the rest of us – with the exception of the cat, which, disgusted, retreated upstairs.

A reluctance to be house-trained was the least of our problems. Once, she chewed up my husband's precious chessmen: heirlooms he had bought when just a boy. Thereafter he refused to speak to Orla for two full days.

We are all besotted with her. She knows just how to get what she wants by placing her soft velvety head on our knees and gazing up with her beseeching brown eyes.

She keeps us fit by encouraging long walks, she makes us laugh with her absurd behaviour (tail-chasing and rolling on chews), and she warms our hearts with her affectionate nature. She has brought so much joy into our lives; to see her dancing through sunlit meadows, chasing the shadows of butterflies, lifts the spirits like nothing else.

Maybe we should have given in to Edward earlier, but we might never have known our beautiful, delightful Orla.

LIKES chasing shadows, rolling in fox poo

DISLIKES not being allowed to eat the cat's food

FINEST HOUR winning my husband over by presenting him with countless abandoned golf balls. (Worst moment: retrieving a player's golf ball that had just landed six inches from the hole)

Christeen Malan, Otford, Kent

Foxy, Sri Lankan beach dog

Foxy's HOME is a large patch of sand in south Sri Lanka, which I first visited five years ago.

She came and sat every night on my terrace. She was

suffering from emaciation and mange, yet was so friendly. She soon realized I was a soft touch, and followed me constantly.

After two days, a bath was due. She had never had one before but she just loved it, and groaned with pleasure.

Next was a visit – by tuk-tuk, no less – to the vet's, where I arranged for her to be treated and spayed.

I then set about fattening her up, and the locals couldn't believe I was giving her steak.

She became my protector, and other dogs couldn't come close. We had hours of cuddles, long walks and the kind of attention, love and fun she had never experienced. I have to admit she even shared the bed.

The sad day came when I had to leave. I cried all the way to Colombo, but arranged with the staff to feed her in return for a monthly fee.

I have been back to the same spot in Sri Lanka every year since, and I only have to walk on the beach when I arrive and whistle, and she is there like a shot, going mad with excitement.

I have often thought about bringing her back here. But she is happy in her familiar world, especially now that she is well fed, healthy and a cut above the other dogs (she is very proud of her collar). She has her own vet, who checks on her every six months, as well as two carers. I have even organized a suitable retirement home for her, for when the time comes.

I simply can't wait till next February to see her again.

LIKES steak and tummy rubs
DISLIKES prawns and fish bones
FINEST HOUR remembering my whistle after twelve months

Stephan Deare-Bilham, Chiswick

Mila, deaf Old English sheepdog

O F THE eight puppies in the litter, why did we go and choose the deaf one? The more we think about it, the more we are certain that it was Mila that chose us.

After taking professional advice, we began the long and patient job of training her to understand a series of hand signals. She soon learnt to look at us for signals, and not to look when she didn't want to obey!

And it was a wonderful feeling, the day we plucked up the courage to let her off the lead in a quiet field, knowing that she had freedom, but would come back to us at the appropriate signal (arms in the air).

She did get totally confused one day in the local park when a lady practising Tai Chi appeared to be giving Mila the 'come here!' signal . . .

Mila is an Old English sheepdog, and we named her after the Casa Mila, a famous building in Barcelona, but we often joke, 'You can call her what you like – she can't hear you!' She is cute and cuddly and has the most gorgeous blue eyes – unusual in a pet, but a sure sign of deafness, we now realize.

People always want to stroke her, and often comment that it is a shame she can't hear, but in reality it is a challenge for us, not for Mila. Fireworks, loud traffic and machinery do not worry her, and of course she sleeps very soundly.

She can totally disarm the most loud and aggressive dogs (or people) with a wag of her tail and a nuzzle of her big black nose.

She doesn't have an ounce of malice in her. Mila, our lovable deaf dog, is the most wonderful, friendly companion – we are so glad she chose us.

LIKES people, dogs, cats
DISLIKES rain, grooming
FINEST HOUR when she wandered onto a nudist beach and discovered a taste for suncream

Sandra Stansfield, Shrewsbury

Teddy, Labradoodle

WE TALKED of having a dog for some time, but there were a few obstacles to overcome. The husband was reluctant, the son had allergies and could I fit the walks in on a busy day with three children to get to school on time? Finally the husband caved in, and so I set about searching for the 'right' dog for us.

Early in 2012 I visited Broadreach Dogs near Cambridge and met Teddy, the F2 miniature Labradoodle. Medium-sized, she assured me, and not likely to shed hair at all, so ideal for my son. Of the puppies, Teddy seemed incredibly laid-back, not bothered if he was chosen or not. Maybe a good sign, I thought.

We brought him home at nine weeks old and he simply fitted in like an old slipper. No crying through the night, just a few little accidents on the floor (only to be expected) and a slight change of lifestyle to accommodate another little person that needed care and attention. But the rewards? Almost too many to mention. A sweet-natured softie that greets us all with a waggy tail every single morning.

From the beginning, I took him with me in his cage in the car, so he's happy to sit and wait during the school pick-up or while I shop. He's not too big when we holiday in our caravan, and is completely relaxed as we head out on our boat for a trip along the coast near East Head.

Teddy was one year old yesterday. The children sang him 'Happy Birthday'. But for me, the best bit is the walking. I never used to walk anywhere – always too busy – so I just took the car. Now I love it. Rain or shine, he's happiest when jumping through long grass looking like a little lamb, trying to catch a hare – and that makes me smile. He's the best decision we made in 2012.

LIKES devouring pigs' ears
DISLIKES a wash in the utility sink
FINEST HOUR being dressed in a Build-a-Bear tutu and revelling in the attention

The Wilson Family, Northamptonshire

Barclay, best friend

BARCLAY, THE best golden retriever that ever lived, did not have a good start to life. I found him at a puppy farm, which I tried in vain to have closed down. He and his siblings were taken away from their mother far too early and were sickly and undernourished.

The vet was not optimistic when he inspected this unhealthy little dog, and gave him a year at most. But with lots of care and monthly hormone injections that I became an expert at administering, he lived until he was thirteen.

When my son Adrian was born, Barclay took it upon himself to be his guardian at all times, parking himself beside the pram or cot and keeping a sharp lookout for any interlopers. He entered into all games with a grandfatherly indulgence, and saw off our other golden retriever, Diggetty, whose favourite diet seemed to be small motor cars, Transformers and pieces of Lego.

Diggetty's dietary requirements also ran to children's food: at Adrian's fourth birthday party, he was caught red-handed, or rather, red-muzzled, paws up on the table, helping himself to all the strawberry jellies and sweets. A howl from the birthday boy and Barclay was in like a flash, dragging the culprit off the table and giving him a headmasterly ticking-off, which resulted in some sulking and skulking on the naughty step while Barclay graciously welcomed the small visitors.

But Barclay's greatest gift was that he could talk. He was a huge hit with my parents. My mother, in between visits, would phone for a chat. She would say, 'Put Barclay on the line.' I would hold the receiver to his ear while she inquired about his health and well-being, and he would answer with a series of snorts and grunts. On arriving home from excursions, we would be greeted with a curled lip and grunted rumblings.

This picture of Adrian and Barclay's tea party is one of my most treasured. I have neither of them any more, but I have wonderful memories.

LIKES biltong (South African dried meat)
DISLIKES loud bangs (not really a retriever, more a human being)
FINEST HOUR emerging from the trees after disappearing for hours at the shock of some clay-pigeon shooting in the area, and being greeted by frantic, tearful owners

Jackie Pilkington, Salisbury

PART SEVEN

PAMPERED CHARMERS

Lupin, the best cat in the world

'CALL ME Lupin.' Actually, he started off as Lulu until he showed us all otherwise. Exchanged for a bottle of champagne, we got him for my son's sixth birthday, and he's remained Joe's cat for twelve years now. He's endured being laughed at openly by a cleaner, who thought his black moustache hilarious, and he's suffered being slung out regularly for hours on end by a visiting American sister-in-law with 'asthma issues' ('He's in the damn house – I just know it'). He used to follow the family into church, but then came the schism: the vicar was happy to have him, but the churchwarden objected, so Lupin got slung out of another joint.

He's very well loved – somehow a touchstone to keep anxiety a little bit further away. Joe has one of his whiskers in an ornate gilt frame in his room at college, a relic. Some months ago, he snapped a tendon in his right front paw and now sits around with one foot off the ground. The vet declared it inoperable. I'm positive they were in it together. There are five flights of stairs in the house, and he gets picked up and taken to various sinks because he refuses to drink still water.

So there are shades of mortality for him, and I get concerned about where we're going to bury him. The garden's not deep enough to ensure he stays under – the previous cat had to be given a showbiz interment in a Zippos Circus skip on Blackheath (there was a council strike on and the dump was closed). It'll be sad to see him go, but it'll be a welcome break for me from being the human palanquin. His headstone will say: *Lupin, the Best Cat in the World. Reader, I carried him.*

LIKES watching snooker
DISLIKES police horses
FINEST HOUR uncanny and intense glaring at sister-in-law from garden bench

Dave Ashmore, Blackheath

Marmaduke, surf dude

WITHIN TWO weeks of moving into our cottage, Colin was off to the cat rescue centre. I arrived home from the hairdresser to find that Marmaduke had been installed. He claimed Marmaduke 'had chosen him'.

The next two or three weeks were absolute hell. Not only was Marmaduke a confident adult cat with a high opinion of himself, he also thought he was in charge. It took a lot of persuasion (and some physical injuries) on our part, but eventually he got the message that he was one of the family, not the team leader. He still lets us know his opinion on most things, but at least not via the medium of teeth and claws.

Marmaduke is a very sociable cat, and loves nothing better than joining in. Three months after he moved in we held a housewarming party. How would he cope? When we tracked him down in the middle of the party he was on the lawn, between two of our friends, wearing my sunhat.

We have since discovered that he has a thing about dressing up, and he now has his own wardrobe. His favourite item of clothing is his Puchi 'Talk to the Paw' diamanté-encrusted T-shirt.

He is so well and truly one of the family that we also take him on holiday, though finding cat-friendly accommodation can be a challenge. He's been to Pembrokeshire and the Peak District, the Cotswolds and the West Country. He's walked on Dartmoor and explored the New Forest; he's even visited some English Heritage properties. We have to watch out for dogs, but the only incident to date is an unprovoked attack on a golden retriever.

Cornwall is his favourite destination as we stay by the sea, so he can go rock-pooling, eat fish and chips and indulge his passion for surfing. You think we're joking.

LIKES sleeping, fish suppers, grooming
DISLIKES our rabbits, rising before four p.m.
FINEST HOUR attending a New Year's Eve party at a neighbour's house

Janette Dollamore and Colin Stenning, Cobham, Surrey

Daisy the chicken

EVERYONE SAYS it's cruel to keep a hen all on its own. My other hens eventually died, and I was going to get her some companions until it quickly became obvious that she was positively thriving as a lone hen. In fact, she's by far the happiest, healthiest hen I've ever had.

True, I'm around most of the time so she has company, and she has the freedom of the garden too. She squawks like mad if I dare to confine her to her palatial run (which is a massive twenty by twenty feet, complete with sand for dust-bathing), so I usually give in and let her wander freely.

She's a real character, and loves trying to terrorize my cats, not to mention the two seagulls who have turned up daily for the past five years for their own tin of cat food, the pigeon collective and a family of pheasants that visit most days. As for the fox, I don't think he'd dare!

She lays daily, and potters about in my office where I play her YouTube films of hens and chicks (she loves the one that plays a song called 'Chicken Train'), and sits on the floor in silence until it's finished.

She knows her name and comes if she's called. She's incredibly curious, and is always up for a new game with a ball or checking out what's in the grocery bags when I arrive back from the supermarket.

The biggest problem is that she will try to eat the cats' food (I put her back in her pen so she doesn't wolf down their biscuits, which she'll do at breakneck speed given half a chance).

I think she loves being a lone hen, and doesn't miss being bullied and pecked by other hens at all, an inevitable and less appealing aspect of keeping hens.

LIKES any food – especially cheese and courgettes – except hen food
DISLIKES not being allowed to sleep on the cats' cushions
FINEST HOUR getting into the car boot and pecking at all the grapes

Barbara Baker, Truro

Myrtle, lovable disgrace

THIS IS Myrtle, a one-year-old miniature wire-haired dachshund. She arrived at our home in Cambridgeshire last summer to join our family of four. She has tan eyebrows to match her paws and chops.

We were going to call her Bertha or Daphne, but my five-year-old son and eight-year-old daughter liked Myrtle, due to some *Harry Potter* character who hangs around in the loos (this should have been an omen, as you will see).

Our old cocker spaniel, Mabel, had just fitted in and caused no trouble. Myrtle, on the other hand, sussed out early on that an entire village was there to fawn over her and that it would be rude not to make the most of it by urinating on every surface in the house, fouling in every room, attempting to eat it and crying and yelping every time I went off to do something upstairs.

Things have improved considerably, and my love for Myrtle has reached a point I thought was only reserved for children. People stop in the street to admire her cuteness. At dinner parties, Myrtle is passed around the table along with the After Eights. Even the most hardy of middle-aged farmers have tickled her tummy while talking about the threat of wind farms.

My husband says that a third child would have needed less clearing up and attention. He has a point, but I can't seem to get enough of her wet nose nudging my hand for tickles, and the joy I get from watching her wedge herself into any open cupboard or welly will never falter.

My husband was never a fan. However, not long ago Myrtle suddenly sat up and looked across the room at him. She then padded across in front of us. He gave her an ear scratch and looked at me with a smug smile. She's no fool, my Myrtle.

LIKES running up to the biggest dog in the park, barking at them and then running away yelping when they turn around to sniff hello
DISLIKES our garden: she treads on it like it's emitting poison
FINEST HOUR working out that she did actually fit in her bed if she moved around ninety degrees

Charlotte Andrews, Cambridgeshire

Cameron, tortoiseshell cat

CAMERON ARRIVED from the cat rescue centre as a tiny scrap of tortoiseshell fur with a snuffle. She had been hand-reared, and for the first few weeks I had to feed her from the tip of my finger. She slept deep in the fur of our other cat, the tolerant Wadworth.

Eventually she lost the snuffle and began to grow, though she was never a large cat. From very early on she became the 'property' of our five-year-old daughter, Laura, an arrangement which seemed to suit them both. She slept on Laura's pillow at night and when, several years later, she discovered how to purr, she would purr only for Laura. She also discovered where Laura went during the day and would make the 200-yard trip to the infant-school playground, searching until she found her. In the summer she would find Laura's classroom and go in to find her, causing havoc.

She had a taste for adventure, and loved travelling in the car. If my husband or I spotted her wandering the streets, all we had to do was open the passenger door. She would jump in and spend the rest of the journey with her back legs on the seat and her front paws on the dashboard, watching the traffic. Everyone knew her in the village, and people we didn't know would tell us where they had seen her.

Cameron had an ambivalent attitude towards dogs. Most she would see off with a cold stare, but once she went home with a family with a Labrador, with whom she spent the night.

LIKES Laura, Laura's pillow, climbing the ladder to Laura's cabin bed, exploring

DISLIKES people who were not Laura (at least during her early years)

FINEST HOUR always being aware of when Laura was in trouble (a not infrequent occurrence) and following her upstairs to her bedroom to offer lots of love and purrs

Rachel Leonard, Bucks

Murphy, Abyssinian cat

INHERITED Murphy as a pet when I met and married his owner, Tony. It was clear from the start that I would have to share my new husband's affections, but it was his unashamed devotion to the gorgeous pedigree Abyssinian that finally convinced me that this was the man for me.

As a tiny kitten, Murphy would climb onto Tony's head, and as he got older he'd sit on his chest, put his front legs around his neck and nuzzle his face. Whether we were entertaining or eating alone, Murphy would join us, jumping onto a spare chair and peering inquisitively over the table. He would never climb on the table or try to take food from our plates, but he was delighted to lick plates and had a gourmet's appreciation of spicy chillies and tagines, although crème fraîche was his favourite.

Typically for Abyssinians, Murphy loved people and wanted to be part of everything that was going on. Once, when we were having new flooring fitted, he got himself trapped under the floorboards. Another tradesman was almost startled into crashing his van when, halfway home from a job, Murphy jumped onto the front seat. He regularly got himself shut in the garage or one of our cars, not to mention his habit of climbing into the tumble dryer onto a heap of warm clothes.

Far from being a 'one man' cat, Murphy was promiscuous with his affections and we discovered that several neighbours, some with cats, were graced by visits (usually rewarded by titbits). The postman, the window cleaner and the deliverers of local church leaflets were all devotees. Murphy strongly disapproved when we left him alone. If we were on foot he'd follow us to the limit of his territory, uttering distress calls to warn us to go no further, and on our return he'd be sitting on the doorstep if the sun was out or, in colder weather, inside on the windowsill watching for us.

He always had a healthy appetite so when, shortly after his thirteenth birthday, he began to go off his food and lose weight, we knew something was seriously wrong. Liver failure was diagnosed, and gradually he became weaker and as winter drew in, spent more and more time in his bed. What a hard decision it was to have him put to sleep, but we knew we had to let him go. I miss his little face looking through the glass panes in the kitchen door every morning. I miss seeing him in the window when I come home, and I miss his warm little body and stroking his silky coat – and those golden eyes looking deeply into mine. Murphy was a little person in a furry coat.

LIKES people, crème fraîche and duvets
DISLIKES power washers and vacuum cleaners
FINEST HOUR frightening off a fox in the garden

Linda Ames, Epping

Snowy, the drama queen

SNOWY, OUR wire-haired Jack Russell drama queen, liked laughter and applause as much as any actress.

She specialized in rubbing the very top of her head on the

carpet, then showing us the resulting 'style'. The more my husband and I laughed, the more the show went on.

At one time we lived in a house backing on to a park. Snowy was adept at squeezing through the hedge, racing across the park, collecting any stray tennis balls from around the courts and streaking back with her treasure. Over time we had several carrier bags full. She played ceaselessly with these balls, potting them with the very end of her nose in a style a snooker player would have envied. Any visitor who was foolish enough to join in would be the first to tire.

We had our suspicions about her evening toilet outings. If it was raining, Snowy would somehow manage to come back through the Jack-Russell-flap completely dry. We set up watch one stormy night, and discovered her secret.

Rather than going for her toilet trip, Snowy stayed immediately outside the flap under the eaves of the bungalow, so that she didn't have to go out into the rain and get wet. We could almost see her counting until she'd decided that enough time had passed and it was safe to re-enter. This she did, shaking herself heartily, and the message was 'no one should send a dog out in that'.

But she hadn't answered the call of nature. As a result, we would then be woken in the night – not by a bark, but a frail, hammed-up cough that said, 'If you don't come soon it'll be too late.' We'd find her with two paws on the edge of her basket and her mouth against the crack in the door for full volume. When she finally went to sleep, she was flanked by tennis balls.

LIKES being the centre of attention
DISLIKES any form of rain
FINEST HOUR retrieving lost tennis balls

Philippa Snow

Gizmo, black smoke Persian

THIRTEEN YEARS ago, I lost a much-loved black Persian rescue cat called Amber. I did not plan to get another cat. That is, until I saw Gizmo.

He was twelve months old, a black smoke Persian cat who needed a new home because his owner was allergic to his fur. He stood on his hind legs like a dog to beg for his dinner, and seemed to be quite a character.

I soon found, however, that he disliked travelling in the car. He howled all the way home.

Friends were coming to dinner, and I was worried how Gizmo would react at first. But I needn't have been concerned. He was very friendly and enjoyed all the attention. He sat in the dining room watching us. All seemed to be going very well until he jumped onto the table, knocking the wine over.

Gizmo is very inquisitive, and stands on his back legs like a meerkat to get a better view of anything going on. He will run to the front door when a visitor arrives to greet them, and then take possession of his favourite chair before they can think of doing so.

The post is another attraction. He will run to the door and

stand on his back legs if it is coming through the letterbox, then sit by it until it is removed by a human being.

Gizmo has to be groomed twice a day. This he will tolerate, and roll over onto his back so his tummy can be combed. He refuses to sleep on his cat bed, and likes instead to sleep on my bed. A gentle pat on the face which becomes more persistent means he wants attention. He is now fourteen years old and is mainly a house cat. He still likes to go into the garden in the summer and hide behind the hydrangeas to see if anything interesting might be happening.

LIKES newspapers and being stroked
DISLIKES travelling in a car – probably because he realizes he is going to the vet
FINEST HOUR chasing a squirrel into the kitchen

Pamela Mann, Wallasey

Smokey and Blue, Russian Blues

INHERITED Smokey and Blue, my four-year-old Russian Blue cats, from a friend. I could not believe my luck to be gifted two felines of such superior quality. They have distinctive plush double coats – silky soft, like the fur of a seal – noble profiles and a slight striping to the tail. Blue wears a blue collar, so that he knows which one he is, but Smokey is happy to model neckwear of any hue. Smokey is the more dominant puss, and perfectly happy as long as he is carried over a shoulder, day and night. Attention-seeking does not begin to describe his behaviour. Blue is aloof; and as the more beautiful of the pair, I feel he is entitled to a slight snootiness.

Smokey has a fondness for 'human' food: pizza or toast and Marmite being his favourites. I am not sure what Blue eats – or indeed where, but he does not dine in our house, and yet he is two pounds heavier than his brother. All I can think is that his beauty allows him access to other houses, where he feasts on shoals of fish and pints of fresh cream.

Blue chirrups and trills at incredible volume. It is easy to get them both purring; sometimes an affectionate look is all that is required, and then, like two grey engines, they rumble and vibrate.

The breed is known for its sympathy. They will pat an owner's face in an attempt to cheer him. But if a visitor calls, the pair of them disappear like sleek grey streaks beneath a loose floorboard, or go crashing out through the cat flap. I have tried to instil some good manners into them, and have explained how rude this behaviour is – but you might as well talk to the cat.

LIKES wailing loudly

DISLIKES cold, wet weather, the bathroom

FINEST HOUR the one and only time they caught a bird. Blue saw a collared dove outside and like a feline Geoff Capes, hurled his full nine-pound weight at my little wooden bird table, deftly breaking it in two

Trish Ellis, London

Harvey, armchair-loving bunny

AMONG HARVEY'S most memorable moments was when someone broke through our computer defences and sent him a letter from Las Vegas, which read: 'Dear Harvey, would you like to explore a career as a forensic scientist or a law enforcement officer?' Maybe not the right post for him, as he loves to be centre stage.

He welcomes all visitors, and loves to show off his Geronimo jump from the sofa. He enjoys watching *The Simpsons*, fringing his favourite armchair cover, pulling off bedsocks and stamping frantically whenever someone peels a banana. He adores his hay bag, cuddles and carrots.

His refusal to recycle his caecotrophs is a bit of a problem, especially first thing in the morning before I put the kitchen light on. Poo on fluffy slippers isn't the ideal start to the day, but this has always been the trouble with Harvey. After consultation with our specialist vet, the pellets were gradually reduced to a minimum with hay and greens. Digestion has improved.

Harvey is now nine. His teeth are good, he has a fine head of hair – which is more than can be said for his human second in command – and he is as active as ever. We live together in bonded harmony, ruled by this rabbit who, with his every growl, teeth-grinding purr, sock-pull and foot-stamp is undoubtedly wanting to be understood.

> **LIKES** visitors
> **DISLIKES** being outdoors
> **FINEST HOUR** having a book dedicated to him: One Hundred Ways to a Happy Bunny by Celia Haddon

Janet Toseland, Northampton

Tamby,
'Tamburlaine the Great', stable cat

TAMBY WAS about eight weeks old when he entered my life in July 1999. My husband came through the door late at night with this little scrap of marmalade in his hand. 'Could have done without that,' he said rather grumpily. We lived in the country, and Tamby had parked himself in the middle of a country lane. My husband stopped the car, opened the door to move the kitten out of harm's way and the next thing he knew it had jumped into the passenger seat.

I opened a small tin of tuna, which Tamby devoured. We had a boxer and a standard poodle and the kitten seemed to be at home with them immediately – he knew he was onto a good thing.

There weren't many other dwellings in the vicinity, but I went the rounds with a notice asking if anyone had lost a marmalade tabby. After a week, the lady who owned the local stables told me three of the stable kittens had gone missing, of which our little bundle was one: would we like to keep it? The little thing had made himself so much at home that I couldn't refuse.

The marriage ended, the dogs died and I was left in a flat with Tamby, who has developed a quirkier character as the years have gone by. There is a saying that 'You own a dog, but a cat owns you.' That is certainly true.

Last year I decided, after much consideration, that I really did want to have a dog back in my life. After waiting six months for a gorgeous Klee Kai, I arrived home after a trip up North to collect him and set up all the paraphernalia – it's like having a new baby. As a result, Tamby refused to eat and after two days, left home. What could I do? It was almost a case of 'droit de seigneur'. The little puppy had to go back to the breeder, and peace was restored with Tamby as 'top dog'.

He has become more proprietorial with the years. I am woken with a gentle tap on the nose, which means he has waited long enough and wants his morning treat. He has commandeered most of the bottom half of my double bed, which means that I have to sleep diagonally across it. I wouldn't change things for the world, and dread the moment when I haven't got my wonderful Tamby to share my life.

LIKES the way he dumps himself between me and any male visitor
DISLIKES the new housemate
FINEST HOUR landing with his 'posterior in the butter' when he found me

Jan Leeming

PART EIGHT

PET THERAPISTS

Rosie, chocolate Labrador, comforter

Nosy Rosie, as she is known in our house – for she always has her elegant nose in something – has proved to be more than just a dog. She is friend, confidante, matron, comedienne, personal trainer and child entertainer. I may be accused of donning Rosie-tinted specs, but let me tell you why I believe Rosie deserves her name in print.

We are bonded by the difficult times in our lives. Hers was being abandoned as a puppy and left on the streets as a stray, and mine coping with a husband serving in three wars: Iraq, Afghanistan and Libya. In eight years of marriage, we have spent many months apart, and it is Rosie's friendship that helps to fill the void of his absence.

When I am upset, she rests her head on my knee to tell me I am not alone. When I anxiously watch the news, she does too, ears pricked to the sounds of gunshots. In 2003, when a

Tornado GR4 was shot down by a patriot missile and I didn't know if it was my husband or not, she never left my side.

She helps out at home, too. If the children fall over and cry, she is the first to get there, licking them better. If I am busy, she plays with them, and you can always count on her to do something silly to make us laugh. If we're not giving her enough attention, she'll lie on her back with her tongue hanging out, playing dead until we do. Once I timed her doing this for fifteen minutes until we gave in.

Rosie does her best to look after us. If the doorbell rings, she assumes her position as protector until she is happy that no harm is intended. She is truly our keeper. She holds us together when times are tough, and her constant zest for life helps to carry us through. When my husband finally walks back through the door, she'll say hello, then allow us time on our own like a thoughtful mother-in-law.

There are many unsung heroes in the strife for peace, and Rosie is one of them.

LIKES exploring, swimming and going to the vet
DISLIKES baths and missing walks
FINEST HOUR all of them

Susie Buchanan, Lincolnshire

Smashie, feline medic

SMASHIE WAS a rescue kitten who was given a home by my wife before she knew me. When I came onto the scene, he was unsure about sharing his home with another man and let me know this on one of the first weekends I stayed. Smashie jumped onto my stomach and walked up to my chest as if coming to be fussed over, but then, quite deliberately, headbutted me and walked off. Having made his point, we then became firm friends.

Some years after we were married, we were woken at four o'clock in the morning by an uneasy sense that all was not well. Smashie was on the bed as usual but, when we switched on the light, we saw blood on the bedspread and one of his front paws badly injured. We think he had been under a car and his paw had been trapped under one of the wheels as the car pulled away from the kerb.

We rushed him to the vet where he underwent emergency surgery and his paw was saved. He came home with a large bandage on his paw, antibiotics and a 'buster collar' to stop him getting to the bandage. We saw him repeatedly headbutting the wall so he could reach the bandage, but apart from that he was a marvellous patient. He went to the vet every few days and became a favourite there. He took his antibiotics and stayed indoors.

A few years later, he returned the favour when I was badly injured in a road accident and fractured both legs and an arm. As soon as I was on the sofa, Smashie jumped on my stomach, walked up to my chest and settled down, purring.

It was the best medicine I could have had.

Smashie took an active interest in my rehabilitation. He enjoyed having a bed downstairs, and slept on it day and night. He also shared the sofa with me, and particularly enjoyed the box set of *The Sopranos*.

LIKES licking butter off breakfast plates
DISLIKES his sleep being disturbed by the hoover
FINEST HOUR his determination in getting to us after his accident, limping to the back door, through the cat flap, up the stairs and onto the bed on three legs, with an injured paw.

Jamie Wallace, Yorkshire

Dexter, Samoyed

DEXTER ARRIVED the day after I had been discharged from hospital following a quadruple heart bypass. I was fifty-five, and a year earlier had undergone two lifesaving operations for cancer.

There I sat, swathed in dressings and struggling to breathe when Dexter made his grand entrance on my daughter's shoulder, looking rather like a large roll of cotton wool that had mysteriously sprouted legs. He looked over at me, his dark brown almond-shaped eyes twinkled and he smiled his Sammy smile. It was love at first sight.

Dexter was eight weeks old and, as I was off work, I was assigned puppy-sitting duties while my daughter was out. These went from ball-throwing and sedately trotting around the garden with him chasing an old towel, to the short strolls that were necessary for my recovery.

Dexter lives with my daughter in a village on the edge of a nature reserve, with the tidal River Crouch running through it. As the weeks went by our short strolls became longer walks, and he discovered a passion for running through thick mud, swimming in the freezing water and eating the occasional decomposed seagull.

He would start his walk with his thick white coat looking beautiful, returning home happy, tramping mud over the carpets and needing a hose down. He became immediate friends with every dog, cat and human he met, and was quite aggrieved if anyone dared ignore him.

Dexter was twelve weeks old when he first found me in the middle of the night. I awoke to see two huge paws on the bed, with his smiley and delighted face just above the mattress. From that time on he shared the bed whenever I stayed at my daughter's house, he on the best part near the window, where he could keep a watchful eye on the street, and me squashed into whatever bit of the bed remained.

Two years on, I have made a full recovery thanks to my wonderful family, medical team, employers and a Samoyed called Dexter.

LIKES stealing socks while you are wearing them
DISLIKES not being the centre of attention
FINEST HOUR leaping over a huge garden fence to see his two terrier friends, even though the gate was open

Angela Curtis, Enfield, London

Furry Friend, tabby cat

Furry Friend appeared during the summer of 2005, and over the next few months became an acquaintance rather than a visitor. Somewhat hesitant to start with, his confidence came to the fore when, in early 2006, my partner Richard was diagnosed with cancer. Richard and Furry Friend male-bonded, and during the summer he spent recovering from the effects of chemotherapy, I would return home after work to find the pair of them asleep in the armchair, Furry Friend nestling on Richard's lap. I didn't get a look-in. And that is how the pecking order has continued.

After about a year, Furry Friend thought nothing of staying the night. His paw was now well and truly 'in the door'.

He has the run of our garden during the day, and continues to maintain that aloof manner only cats possess.

Not known for his endearing nature (his background remains a mystery to us), his demonstrative affections are limited to the armpit nuzzle and the headbutting nudge.

The cold winter of 2010 to 2011 saw Furry Friend take up

permanent residence. During his first visit with us to a vet for a skin complaint in August this year, we found out he was microchipped. Several weeks and one letter later, we officially owned him.

His original name, Moppett, has been replaced by Stripes, but he will always be known as Furry Friend because that's what he was in Richard's hour of need.

LIKES roast chicken, the sun on his face and ambushing ankles

DISLIKES Maurice, one of our neighbours, Snowy the hissing cat and tin foil

FINEST HOUR bringing in a decapitated squirrel as a present

Kay West, Birmingham

Dexter, cocker spaniel

ROBBIE THE rabbit had been dead for about two and a half days when our children Richard and Eleanor's tears turned into pleas: 'Can we have a dog now?' We had always used Robbie as an excuse not to go along that path, and the children's sorrow turned to joy as realization dawned – that hurdle had hopped off to the great hutch in the sky.

Eleanor, then twelve, had been the most vocal. Not a day went by without a promise to walk a dog, to feed him, to clear up after him. Slowly we were worn down and Dexter came into our lives. To be fair, it was love at first sight for all of us. He is the most gorgeous tricolour cocker, who has proved to have the loveliest nature.

His only fault is his greed. He will sniff out a picnic from a mile away, and many a time we were just too slow and a chicken leg or pork pie would disappear from a startled family's hamper.

Eleanor was as good as her word and walked Dexter and taught him tricks. Despite 'not being allowed upstairs', he was often snuggled up on her bed as she pored over homework. If she was in the house, the rest of us didn't get a look-in.

In March 2009, Eleanor, then fourteen, was walking with friends when a driver lost control of his car and mounted the pavement. She died four days later.

We all now realize why Dexter came into our lives. In those first days of grief and shock, he gave us routine. We felt like shutting ourselves away, but we had to walk him and face people. Whenever anyone visited to offer their condolences, he broke down any awkwardness. People would be struggling to find words of comfort and the ice would be broken by a spaniel humping their leg!

He would sneak upstairs but, poignantly, would not enter her bedroom – just lie outside her open door. Two years later, and he accompanies us to our nearby churchyard every day and sits quietly by her grave. His ability to judge our mood is amazing. Life moves on, and we have had to learn to carry on without our daughter, but if we ever feel down, he is on our lap immediately. A bracing walk with him is the best therapy.

We are so grateful that Eleanor wore us down four years ago, as we are not sure how we could have coped without him. Some things are just meant to be.

LIKES food – both his own and anybody else's
DISLIKES animals on the television
FINEST HOUR saving our sanity

Gillian McGrath, Essex

PART NINE

HUNTERS AND GATHERERS

Bella, pursuer of pheasants

THE FIRST smooth fox terrier that I owned was called Bella. She had a brown, well-marked head and her bright, intelligent eyes were rimmed with black markings that gave the appearance of exotic kohl make-up. She looked as though butter wouldn't melt in her mouth. One of our daughters bought a name-tag in the shape of a heart, inscribed with 'Bella' and our telephone number. It hung from her collar like a piece of jewellery.

Training went well. Bella was allowed off the lead and came back to heel with the promise of a biscuit. What a good dog, and well behaved.

But one day it all went wrong. A pheasant started up in the field before her and fluttered and fumbled its way back towards the woods with Bella in hot pursuit. I shouted and ran after her, but biscuits and praise were no longer of any interest. In the dark of the woods I could hear birds calling hysterically and thrashing about in the undergrowth. There was no sign of my dog. But then she came out of the trees, hot, panting and triumphant, with an extremely large hen pheasant clamped firmly in her jaws. And, as it is with terriers, she would not let go. I had to walk the length of the village with my small dog determinedly carrying her very large, dead pheasant. I breathed a sigh of relief once inside our garden gate. No one had seen us.

My husband was impressed. The bird was prepared and eaten – delicious. We had got away with it! But the following day, the head of the local shooting syndicate phoned.

'Bella there?' he asked. 'She's left her heart on a branch outside the pheasant pen!'

LIKES lying on her side with all four paws strategically placed against the Aga
DISLIKES travelling in the car
FINEST HOUR catching the pheasant

Rosemary Atkinson, Bath

Rufus, rescue cat

LIKE A mother deluded by love for her son, I thought Ru, as he was nicknamed, was the innocent victim in his many fights, but the vet always reckoned him to be a 'bruiser'. When we first met he was a tiny rescue kitten with huge alien ears. He was plopped unceremoniously into a cardboard carrier and we took him home like a takeaway with lashing claws. With hindsight, he always had the makings of being neurotically territorial. Over the years he perfected a scary bantam-cock strut, but privately he was into cuddling and sucking jumpers.

While young, he became dangerously ill with hepatitis, and his chances were slim. The adult cats in the village took turns watching over him, and one critical day, when he'd refused every food we could think of giving him, a big male cat came and caught a bird for him, which he ate, and which may have been the turning point.

That hot summer cats came and went, checking on their invalid friend – something none of them had done before – and, after his miraculous recovery, never did again.

There weren't many people he liked. He had dreadful manners, spitting with contempt at neighbours, but to me he was loving and special. He trailed me loyally, barely left my side if I was ill and took pleasure in bringing me gifts – birds, mice, shrews and once, a bat. One summer he acquired a new friend – a tiny wild baby rabbit. I got sporadic reports of their unlikely marriage until eventually the bunny vanished and Ru came in with a look I had got to know rather well – it said: 'Anyone asks, bud, you know nothing . . .'

LIKES playing football in the kitchen with balls of tin foil
DISLIKES punks on his turf
FINEST HOUR alerting me to a burglar in the house

Jill Maughan, Co. Durham

Madge and Mabel, the twins

IT WAS love at first sight: two gorgeous black bundles in a litter of ten Staffy/Labrador/whippet crosses from Animal Rescue. Our lovely dog Molly had just died, and we were in desperate need of doggy comfort. But, as we found out to our cost, ne'er buy twins. From day one, they were in charge. We were besotted, and oh were they naughty! We have done so much dog training it is coming out of our ears, and we have finally achieved results. They can be very obedient. But it's hard work, as they are always a jump ahead.

Madge (short for Madonna), certainly lives up to her name. She is beautiful, but she is also bossy and has to be in charge. She is a keen swimmer, and appears to be training for the Olympics, as she practises most days in the stream at our park. She fetches the ball for Mabel, who does not like getting out of her depth.

Mabel is more timid, very loving and yet a killer. Squirrels are her number one interest; she has killed six and has the battle scars to prove it. We spend so much money at the vet that we joke that they could retire on our contributions alone.

Believe it or not, they can both tell the time. They know precisely when it is four o'clock and time for dinner. They also recognize the music at the end of programmes such as *Casualty* and *Silent Witness*, as that's when it's time for biscuits. They come running.

They race each other around the garden, and have tried very hard to ruin our prize lawn and flowers, so we built a fenced-off racetrack.

The twins continually make us laugh. We have so much fun that we could never be without them.

LIKES food, swimming, sunshine and radiators (Madge); being outside, hunting, sunshine and radiators (Mabel)
DISLIKES squirrels and cats (Mabel)

Jane Walker, Leicestershire

Casper, thief

THEY SAY that imitation is the most sincere form of flattery, but I really wish our dog, Casper, didn't take it to heart quite so literally. Let's face it – Casper is a thief. At the beginning of the year he was pinching a few broad beans off the stalk, but as the year has gone on it's been the runner beans, and the tomatoes in the greenhouse if you are careless enough to leave the door open. Now he has been beadily watching us pick anything edible in the garden.

Lately, I have been carefully hiding from him the fact that there were a few courgettes that hadn't turned to marrows. When I went indoors, however, he pounced. But he mistook the bed from where I had picked the courgettes for the one next door, and helped himself to a whole raw beetroot belonging to the neighbour.

Really, is nothing sacred? Mind you, it's always been the same. Some years ago, I greeted my daughter, who I don't see very often, with, 'Hello, darling – come in, I've made a cake . . .

Oh – half a cake.' The other half was under the table, half eaten.

Last Christmas, having been asked to make a Christmas cake for a great friend, I had to excuse the strange shape of the finished article, saying that I was 'experimenting', when actually a great wedge of it had been stolen from the spare-room shelf!

He's really a big softie, though. Some four years ago, when his 'mentor', our other springer, died, he visibly went into mourning. He wouldn't eat, and became an 'old man' almost overnight. So we got him another 'rescue' springer as a companion. Although he was a bit fed up with having a woman around the house, he perked up, and they are now inseparable, although he wouldn't admit it!

LIKES vegetables

DISLIKES having his ears brushed

FINEST HOUR capturing a pigeon in full flight, and then not knowing what to do with it

Pippa Pettifer, Devon

Hector the Hungry

IT WAS a dark and stormy night, shortly before Christmas 2007, when Hector the Hungry appeared in my garden. I could hear him but could not see him, despite my torch. Every time I approached, he melted into the darkness. I gave up, thinking it must be the tabby belonging to a neighbour. But next morning, when I went to feed the birds, he reappeared and started to eat the bird food. I began feeding him, and within days he had moved in. He was about eighteen months old, a large, underweight, affectionate and friendly lost cat.

I would have been heartbroken to lose such a magnificent beast. So I tried for months to trace his owners – he was not microchipped. But despite putting up posters, placing newspaper ads and uploading his picture on a lost-and-found website, his owners never came forward. Then I tried to rehome him, but after six months I realized he was a fixture, and a very welcome one at that.

He's a Just William sort of a cat, a swaggering, bumptious hayseed. When he comes in, I can track his progress through the house from the twigs, leaves and mud he trails in his wake – he is semi-long furred. He frequently brings in live mice and drops them once he is bored, leaving my old deaf cat Hamish to deliver the coup de grâce. This autumn, he has even brought in two large slugs – the brown ones with the orange frills – on his fur and dropped them on the kitchen floor. Worse, he appeared in bed in the early hours recently with a large one encased in the fur on his stomach – the first time I've shared my bed with a slug.

He's very brave, unless another cat stands up to him, when his bravado evaporates. But he is adept at catching young rats (several neighbours keep chickens, which have boosted our local rat population).

And last year he became a blood donor at my local veterinary hospital. So far, he has donated twice. One recipient was severely anaemic as a result of a flea infestation, and the other had liver problems. Both are now back on their feet, with Hector's blood coursing through their veins.

It is the first time I've had a young cat for several years and he has been a joy, full of playfulness and joie de vivre. He weighs in now at 4.5 kg and has huge feet – one of his would make three of those of my delicate silver tabby, Dido.

LIKES being cuddled and having his tummy rubbed
DISLIKES his companion Hamish who, despite being half his size, bullies him
FINEST HOUR becoming a blood donor

Jasmine Profit, Somerset

Dino, red setter, rabbit chaser

DINO WAS a six-month-old Irish setter given to my ex-wife after his first owners sent him back to the breeder. They said he was giving the youngest child epileptic fits. He was named after Dino Ferrari, or so I was told; I think it was more likely the pet dinosaur in *The Flintstones*.

I took him to live with me in the sergeants' mess on an army aviation base at Netheravon, not easy as I was aircrew, but no one said anything. He grew up with helicopters and spent his early years chasing and dispatching rabbits along the airfield perimeter while I was flying, or with me on small-arms ranges.

He had a natural gun dog's instincts; sometimes he would scare up a pheasant then turn and look at me as if to say, 'Are you going to shoot that bird, or what?'

Flying did not bother him. He would jump on board a Lynx, look for a comfy spot such as someone's bag, and go to sleep.

When I was posted back to Northern Ireland for another two-year tour, he obviously could not go with me. My father then looked after him: I believe that walking Dino extended Dad's life. Dino would sit, bring his head back and howl as my dad played blues music on a harmonica.

Once a month I would come home on leave, but I hated leaving him. He would go mad on seeing me, but at the end of my visit would sulk with his head on the parcel shelf of the car and not look at me at all as we returned to the airport.

As an ex-rufty-tufty soldier, I cried my heart out when he had to be put to sleep at the age of twelve. I still miss him.

LIKES blues music, doggy chocolates, Christmas crackers

DISLIKES any small furry things such as cats, rabbits, wild birds

FINEST HOUR stalking a rabbit on his belly for twenty minutes using the only available cover: a small red fire extinguisher

Paul Crooks, St Helens, Merseyside

PART TEN

DEARLY DEPARTED

Oliver, the Peter Pan of dogs

WE WENT for a walk one day, Oliver and I, when the dew was still on the grass and only a few dog walkers roamed the fields around our home. Bounding like a gazelle, his energy was a joy to behold, his dappled colours of red and white catching the morning rays.

I bought him when he was seven months old, all legs and bewilderment. His owner, a lady in Rotherham, couldn't cope; a common thing with setters, due to their free spirit.

Red and whites were, I'm told, the original Irish setters, but breeders phased out the white, presumably as it wasn't conducive to hunting, but you can often see them in old hunting scenes.

Oliver's instincts for retrieving clearly show on his walks, as he always needs to carry a branch or stick, the larger the better.

He could never have been a gun dog, being scared of his own shadow, but he has made up for his shortcomings by becoming our soulmate.

Having had a red setter, I knew that the breed are a challenge, and Oliver has been no exception. I remember one episode when, in a desperate attempt to get him to come back to me, I had to take his food bowl up to the field. But gradually he calmed down to the sensitive and affectionate creature we know and love.

Alas, my walk was a solitary experience this morning as Oliver is no more, reaching his journey's end in February this year. The beauty of setters is that they are the Peter Pan of dogs and never actually grow old, but we miss him like crazy.

LIKES his family, cheese
DISLIKES black dogs, loud noises, the vet
FINEST HOUR his first time on Harlech beach, when he was so overjoyed with the space he barked himself hoarse

Lesley Miller, Worcestershire

Charlotte, traffic warden

OF ALL the cats I have had, the oddest and most lovable was Charlotte, whom I got from the Cats Protection Society.

As far as information is available, she came from an ideal home with a loving mistress. After her owner's death, Charlotte was a stray for nigh on three years and must have suffered much, especially in winter.

Eventually, she got run over and lost nearly all her teeth. She could not groom herself properly, and I'd take her to the vet for grooming every so often.

Charlotte loved all creatures and immediately made contact with half a dozen local cats – in fact, she opened a sort of club, inviting all and sundry to her table, often for big eats.

She spent much of her time in warm weather on a cushion on the garden seat under the cherry tree with her friend the blackbird, who wandered under the seat picking up seed scattered for his benefit.

Charlotte also had her own traffic control! She would walk in a dignified manner down the centre of the highway and let the traffic settle to the side – which it frequently did. She would sometimes stroll over to a car, stand up and receive a stroke and hello before turning down the path.

Sadly, Charlotte died (she had deteriorated over some months). She was a few weeks off twenty, and had certainly lived an active life. One evening, she asked to be picked up – I nursed her; she purred then later cried, the only cat I have ever known to do so. I put her to bed at midnight.

She was still breathing but was gone by four in the morning. The vet had her cremated, and she is still with me, never to be forgotten.

LIKES her friend the blackbird, other cats
DISLIKES the cold
FINEST HOUR her traffic-calming measures

George Henry Underwood, Forest Row, East Sussex

Flint, Great Dane

THIS IS a story of Flint, our incredibly handsome but stubborn-as-a-mule blue Great Dane. My first dog, he came into our lives at eight weeks old with his direct stare and 'Nora Batty' stockinged legs. In his first year, he grew into the long-legged head-turner that earned his photo on tourist cameras from Canada to Japan.

Flint was the firstborn of his litter; he trained well and would do almost anything, but if he decided that he didn't want to, he'd plant his feet and that was it. Try picking up ten stone of Dane! At six months, he picked a fight with a swan in a pond and after fifteen minutes of swimming, guess who had to wade waist-deep in stinking water to haul him out? At nine months, he broke from his lead to chase a sheep, and fell ninety feet over a cliff at the Worm's Head – and walked away with only scratches!

But he could be so gentle. Surrounded by a class of thirty six-year-olds, he would stand and take the pats until an anguished look would say, 'Can we please go now?' Babies would be stepped over after having being inspected and deemed safe. Small dogs were beneath contempt, and large ones received a hard stare. He attracted attention whenever he ventured out, gaining fans.

His finest hour was on the steep, narrow streets of Mont St Michel; I might as well have had a leopard on a lead for the effect as the crowds parted, flattening themselves against walls as Flint passed with the arrogance of a medieval prince.

At nine years old, he was diagnosed with dilated cardio-myopathy, and so began a drug regime that kept him alive but ultimately affected his appetite, and thus his condition. His hind legs became weakened, so we got him a 'chariot'.

With his wheels, nothing would stop him – he'd run over the foot of anyone that got in the way, as spatial awareness could be a problem. Four months after my father had passed away following a massive stroke, Flint, aged eleven years and four months, suddenly collapsed – with a massive stroke. I think I grieved as I had never grieved before.

LIKES food, especially stolen sandwiches

DISLIKES fireworks and gunshots

FINEST HOUR stealing a pork chop; frightening the French

Phillip Hayes, Ramsgate

Safie, mongrel

SAFIE AND her brother were the result of an illicit liaison between her very proper beagle mother and a feral Labrador. Dogs were not on our agenda, but our neighbour was desperate for someone to give a home to the puppies, so we succumbed.

Safie developed into a strangely put-together dog: a small but pretty head, with beautiful ears, sat at the front of a large, coffee-table-like body – all supported on four short, thin legs.

We lived on top of a hill in the Tarn region of France with ten acres of land and a vineyard next door. Safie was in heaven.

The beagle in her meant that she was prone to roam, and would sometimes return with a damaged tail or a burn on her nose. Between walks she would alternate lazing in the sun with the burying of bones.

Every autumn she would help to harvest the grapes and blackberries, eating them straight from the vine and bush.

Over the next few years, Safie travelled everywhere with us, sharing our caravan. She was selective with strangers, preferring to keep her distance – unless food was involved.

She was also anxious with other animals, sometimes with good cause. Torquay Thomas, a cat belonging to our younger daughter, would chase her and make her cry, and even Austin, our older daughter's geriatric chinchilla, would get at her given the chance.

We moved back to England to live in west Dorset four months ago. The woods behind our house soon became Safie's favourite place to walk.

She took to running around in circles when she knew we were going for a walk. She had finally learnt to hold her lead in her mouth instead of tripping over it. A perfect day would end with excavating, then gnawing, an ancient bone on the grass by the garden wall, always the same spot.

Not deterred by the hard frost in December, she was busy gnawing when she spotted a fox in the garden and, uncharacteristically, took chase, jumping the wall behind it. A passing car swerved to miss the fox but hit Safie, killing her.

The next morning, the outline of her shape on the grass was still unfrosted, and her bone lay where she had dropped it. That is where we have buried her. She was such a good dog; she even converted my husband into a dog lover.

LIKES being outdoors and burying bones

DISLIKES any sort of water

FINEST HOUR sitting on our hilltop, guarding her terrain

Cheryl Ashburn, Longburton

Hattie, French bulldog

A FRIEND in Kent, who breeds French bulldogs, gave us Hattie, as she was not show material and needed to go to a good home. For the next fourteen and a half years, Hattie transformed our lives; she was such a character.

She enjoyed chasing squirrels and birds. One day, when out for a walk, she tore after a seagull and, not looking where she was going, inadvertently launched herself quite a long way out into Chichester harbour, not seeing the end of the grass. She surfaced, looking surprised, and managed to turn around and swim back to dry land.

When we went on holiday, my mother loved having her to stay, but on two occasions she disgraced herself – once by eating my mother's false teeth, which must have been taken out and placed within Hattie's reach (a few odd teeth were found on the carpet). The second time was by hurling herself through the glass panel in my mother's front door to get at the postman. Hattie was unhurt, but the postman was shocked. He then had to find a neighbour to look after her as my very deaf mother was still fast asleep.

Hattie hated letters coming through the door, which she regarded as an invasion of her territory. We had to build an outside letterbox after discovering a slightly bloodstained letter, possibly from the postman's fingers! Hattie also managed to destroy several letters before we could rescue them.

Our grandchildren came late into Hattie's life, but despite never having had anything to do with small children, she was marvellous with them, and happy to let them curl up with her in her basket and crawl around the kitchen while she was eating.

Later in life Hattie had corneal ulcers, resulting in five days of blindness. She never lost her love of, or faith in us during this time, and eventually her sight returned.

Her back legs finally gave out, and she was put to sleep cuddled up on the sofa between us, her nightly place when we all watched TV. Five years on, not a day goes by that we don't miss her.

LIKES sharing the sofa, lodged between us
DISLIKES squirrels
FINEST HOUR harbour diving

John and Lynn Hooper, Chichester

✳ ✳ ✳

Tatters, Yorkie

MY FATHER-IN-LAW had decided to buy our three young children a puppy. He had seen a Yorkshire terrier, and would pay all expenses. I didn't really want a dog, but my husband thought it would be good for the children. So Tatters entered our lives.

I fell in love with him immediately – he was so sweet, perky and full of life – but at the time I was a busy mother getting over appendicitis, and had no experience of dogs.

Tatters was clever and soon got the better of me, however. He would steal the children's toys to run off with upstairs, or hide behind the sofa, only to let go of the toy if he was given a treat.

At children's parties he would run off with the dice or – even worse – the parcel from 'pass the parcel'. An unsuspecting child with a biscuit was an easy target.

Tatters was always escaping from the garden: his favourite route was by climbing up the wire fence. Once at the top, his weight would bend the fencing and he would jump down. There was no way he would come back unless caught or given a sausage.

The children loved Tatters, dressing him up in a Cub's cap and scarf or T-shirt, giving him rides in the doll's pram. At Christmas, his basket would be decorated with paper chains and a stocking.

Sadly, as Tatters got older, he grew more difficult and demanding, to the extent that we discussed getting rid of him – but of course we couldn't. He died quite suddenly, with a throat tumour, aged thirteen years. It was a very sad day.

LIKES food
DISLIKES obedience
FINEST HOUR dressing up

Sue Hare, Billericay, Essex

Sybil the sleuth

SYBIL CHOSE us. We were living just outside Brisbane on five acres, and decided to get a puppy. We had been told of a Border collie breeder close by whose bitch had just had puppies, so we went to view them. While watching them all playing, one puppy came up to us and started chewing my husband's shoelaces.

When we asked the breeder whether this particular puppy had been reserved, she replied that she hadn't and that, because of her pricked ears, she wouldn't be able to show her in competitions. We only wanted a pet, so that didn't bother us one iota.

Six weeks later, we picked up Sybil. She was loving, very docile and beautiful, despite those pricked ears! And extraordinarily intelligent. Her pièce de résistance came one Sunday afternoon when we couldn't find the car keys.

My husband had cleaned the car prior to us going out. When it was time to leave, he couldn't find the keys. We looked everywhere and, in the end, had to give up and use the other set. As soon as we got home we searched the dustbins, the shelves in the garage – anywhere else we thought he might have put them. Sybil was following us round. I looked at her and said jokingly, 'If you were a bloodhound you'd find our keys for us.' She looked up at me, turned round and walked to the edge of the garden bed and stared into the grass. There they were! My husband and I looked at each other with our mouths open in amazement. It was as if Sybil had understood every word.

Sadly, at the age of thirteen, Sybil was diagnosed with a tumour on her liver and the vet said that she probably had only a few weeks to live. Six months later, she was still alive but was acting as if she had dementia, and we discussed the option of having her put to sleep because she was so confused. The vet came to our home to give her euthanasia, and she was buried beside a passion-flower plant.

LIKES any type of food but especially fruit
DISLIKES nothing
FINEST HOUR finding those car keys

Maggie Osborne, Thakeham, West Sussex

Gemma, swimmer

A s Gem was a cross, I had the best of two worlds. The collie half was intelligent and obedient, and the lurcher half gentle, calm and trustworthy. She loved to chase in the woods, but lacking the killer instinct, as soon as she got within grabbing distance, she stopped. Even when she accidentally managed to catch a rabbit, she let it go. When our old dog helped herself to Gem's dinner while she was eating it, she backed off instantly as if to say, 'You have that, I didn't really want it anyway,' and then looked at me for help.

I could leave her sitting outside the cake shop, holding her own lead in her mouth. When friends' dogs forgot where they had dropped their balls, I could point in the general direction and say, 'Bring it,' and she would go off and find them.

The collie half of her loved to learn. She knew so many tricks, and she won her Kennel Club Good Citizen Gold Certificate.

She could even carry raw eggs. We were briefly in a dog display team, until one day the lurcher half of her looked up at me in the arena and virtually said, 'You know I can do this, why do I have to keep proving it?' I realized that it wasn't fun for her any more, so we stopped.

What was fun for her was her weekly swim. Usually a peaceful traveller, as soon as she saw me get out her stripy towel, she went into hyper-excited mode. In the car, instead of lying quietly, she went into a tense crouch, peering over my shoulder through the windscreen, panting and talking to herself. Woe betide me if I got caught up in any traffic, because she would complain bitterly (and loudly). It wasn't so much the swimming she liked as the splat she made, hurtling into the water.

Sadly, my beautiful Gemma died recently. I will always remember the way she lived her life.

LIKES weekly 'swim-swim'
DISLIKES loud noises
FINEST HOUR fetching me when my old dog fell into a pond

Sue Ajax-Lewis, West Sussex

Elsa, tortoiseshell cat

I was brought up in Kenya, so when I was given a gorgeous tortoiseshell kitten by a neighbour back in England, I had to call her Elsa. She was such a character, very playful, and I adored her. When Elsa was barely one year old she became pregnant. The day she went into labour she just wanted me to carry her around. Eventually I put her in the prepared maternity unit, a cardboard box with towelling in a corner of our en suite.

Unfortunately, her first kitten was stillborn, but she soon had two more and after cleaning them both, she settled down for the night.

Next morning I happened to be in our en suite, and realized she had just given birth to another kitten, thirteen hours after the others.

Then one morning I was suddenly aware of a cold, wet nose

next to my arm and woke up to see that Elsa had brought all three kittens onto my bed for me to look after while she went outside. Twenty-five years later, it still brings tears to my eyes when I think of the trust she had in me. We had great fun watching the kittens grow up. When they were a few months old we found good homes for them and had Elsa neutered.

Elsa and I had a great relationship, and I am sure she understood a lot of what I said to her (though my husband pooh-poohs this). She loved playing games in the sitting room, hide and seek and tearing after a ping-pong ball – in fact, she would often push the ball back to me.

She was nineteen when she was too frail to carry on and we had her put to sleep. I was heartbroken, and still think of her, but I have been blessed with a beautiful painting of her looking down on me as I sit in 'our' favourite chair where most evenings Elsa would sit on my lap.

LIKES drinking water from the kitchen tap
DISLIKES other cats
FINEST HOUR becoming a 'queen'

Deidre Hilbourne

Sheba, school dog

OFSTED HADN'T been thought of when Sheba the Dalmatian joined the roll of Holywell School, Loughborough where I was headteacher. Every morning, she jumped out of the car, said 'hello' to the little ones also waiting to start their school day, and then curled up either in the office or the cloakroom until morning assembly was over and it was time to do her morning rounds. She visited every class, checking on standards and behaviour and, when satisfied that all was as it should be, her lower lip would curl into a smile.

During breaks, she would be walked by willing volunteers, who also ensured that she didn't starve at lunchtime by collecting leftover scraps. This was a chore taken seriously, but went awry the day I was delayed at a meeting and didn't return until mid-afternoon. I was assured that Sheba had been properly looked after. Yes – she had been given twelve hard-boiled eggs! The children's maths proved correct when Sheba parted company with lunch in the car on the way home.

Sheba had two litters, and when the pups were six weeks old, they spent a day in the open-plan library where they could be seen by everyone. Dodie Smith's novel really came to life then. Sheba had such a lovable nature that we kept Dodger, her son from the second litter, but this was to bring unplanned sadness. Dodger came back from a routine visit to the vet with the then practically unknown illness of parvovirus. He died within days, and Sheba was obviously suffering as well. For over a month she lingered close to death, but was kept alive by my wife's gentle stroking and comforting words, encouraging her to fight and stay with us. It was a joyous moment when I returned from school to be met by a very tottery Sheba, who greeted me with her trademark smile. We all smiled too, and wept happily, realizing she was over the worst.

Sheba was to live another six years, but was no longer strong enough to return to school, so she was marked absent from then on. Even today, former pupils – now grown up and with children and dogs of their own – stop and speak with affection of the school's pet. Sheba was fun, a perpetual teenager and a devoted companion.

LIKES children and going on residential stays with them, especially to Snowdonia
DISLIKES the polished surfaces of the school halls
FINEST HOUR overcoming parvovirus

Clive Williams, Loughborough

Rolly, back-seat singer

OUR FRIENDS, Roger and Val, bought Rolly as a puppy in 1995, so we knew him from early on. Whenever we would visit, this mad bundle of energy would rush around the room; he was never still.

After a divorce, Rolly stayed with Roger, but his health was declining and he asked us to take care of the dog if anything ever happened to him. When Roger died, we kept our word.

Once at home, he was confronted with Tiggy, our old blind cat. Tiggy spent the first two weeks upstairs until she finally plodded purposefully into the lounge, only to be confronted by a confused Rolly, whose experience with cats was limited. His inquisitive nose in Tiggy's face was too much for her, and a well-aimed paw and the resultant yelp from Rolly restored the cat's supremacy.

We took Rolly on his first holiday to a cottage in Devon and he was like a dog released.

The sight of the wind flowing through his fur on the boat made the other passengers smile. He also discovered that ponds are made of water and that, despite looking solid, you can't actually walk on them.

We took him away every year, mainly to the Cotswolds, but also to France, where he was popular among the children, who had never seen a dog like him. They seemed to think he was a lamb.

We live near to a wonderful dog-friendly country-house hotel, and we got into the habit of turning up for Sunday-morning coffee and a walk around the lake. On the journey there, Rolly would start to sing in the back of the car as it was by far his favourite place. In 2010 the old fella had the first of a few mini-strokes that slowed him down, and, at the age of sixteen and a half, we finally had to have him put down. We had him for a wonderful six and a half years.

LIKES chocolate brownies
DISLIKES other dogs
FINEST HOUR the first time he realized he could run flat out, unfettered

John and Pam Simons, Bexhill, East Sussex

Basil, retired athlete

BASIL FOUND us, via the pet-rescue column in the local newspaper. We'd recently taken on a bed-and-breakfast business, and my stepsons had started calling my husband Basil, after Basil Fawlty. He was meant for us. No big decisions over breed, size or colour. One telephone call, one walk, one inspection and he was home before the foot-and-mouth outbreak.

He wasn't keen on the resident cat, Jessie, and, at twenty, she wasn't keen on him, but she licked him into shape and he understood that she was boss. At the same time, he licked us into shape and we understood he was boss.

Basil settled well into his dual role of chief host and security officer at the B & B. He took both roles seriously: he knew he was on a treat bonus scheme, particularly if he got a mention in the visitors' book. If invited, he joined guests for breakfast, partaking of three courses: cereals; the full English, heavy on the bacon and sausages, light on the tomatoes and mushrooms; followed by toast – wholemeal, of course. He was always happy to take guests on a tour of the area, so long as he could include a visit to the park for a game of ball, all part of the duties of a B & B dog.

In his early days he was a dreadful thief – half a pound of butter, a leg of lamb; even the mustard and chilli sandwiches didn't deter him.

Basil was an athlete. He did everything at high speed: every walk, run or swim at 100 per cent.

After undergoing cruciate ligament operations on his back legs, he retired from competitive ball-chasing and took to the water – rivers, the sea – winter or summer, he'd be in.

We lost Basil a few weeks ago to cancer of the throat. He's now in doggy heaven, where the bowl is never empty and walks never end. We miss him a lot; he was our best friend.

LIKES playing ball, swimming, long muddy walks, fruit
DISLIKES vacuum cleaners, bananas, hosepipes
FINEST HOUR being a good friend to my late brother-in-law, who had learning difficulties

Ann Winter, Worcester

Rupert, Love Bug

RUPERT (NAMED after Prince Rupert, who led the cavalry of King Charles I) entered our lives as a very small, very quiet Blenheim Cavalier King Charles spaniel. Not small for very long – I should have known by the size of his paws – and not so quiet. From day one he came to the office with me, where he held court in his basket under my desk. He soon became a firm favourite with everyone; my boss called him 'the sleeping partner'. At lunchtime, Rupert and I walked in Greenwich Park, where he became well known, and also in a lot of the pubs in the area. A Finnish intern we had in the office took him for a walk, and when she came back she said that he had dragged her into a wine bar. All the barmaids in there spoilt him and called him 'Rupert Love Bug'.

We took Rupert with us on holidays, and after he was microchipped and rabies tested he came with us to France five times. Of course in France, dogs are allowed in bars, restaurants and hotels. Rupert would sit with us in a five-star restaurant looking very demure, but eyeing up the steak at the next table.

He was a good-looking dog, and had a presence about him. He did seem to be attractive to other dogs, and lady dogs in the park would fuss over him. Rupert did his George Clooney impression – aloof but sexy. He was also very greedy. One day we were having a dinner party, and when I went into the dining room I noticed that the cheese was missing from the sideboard – guess who. On another occasion, a friend was staying with us and Rupert stole from her, and devoured, a whole box of chocolate liqueurs.

Sadly, Rupert had a heart condition and at ten years and three months we lost him; at least he passed away at home with us. We buried him in the grounds of our estate, in the company of thirty neighbours and three dog friends. I read Lord Byron's elegy to his dog Boatswain. We still remember and miss him – he was a delightful companion and a good friend.

LIKES swimming in the sea on a hot day
DISLIKES getting his paws cold in the snow
FINEST HOUR finding and eating the chocolate Easter eggs from an Easter-egg hunt some children were having on Ramsgate beach

Eleanor Clark, Greenwich